AF412179

This series offers the concerned reader basic guidelines and *practical* applications of religion for today's world. Although decidedly Christian in focus and emphasis, the series embraces all denominations and modes of Bible-based belief relevant to our lives today. All volumes in the Steeple series are originals, freshly written to provide a fresh perspective on current—and yet timeless—human dilemmas. This is a series for our times. Among the books:

How to Read the Bible
James Fischer

Soulwinning: An Action Handbook for Christians
Reg A. Forder

A Spiritual Handbook for Women
Dandi Daley Knorr

Temptation: How Christians Can Deal with It
Frances Carroll

*With God on Your Side: A Guide to Finding
Self-Worth Through Total Faith*
Doug Manning

*A Daily Key for Today's Christians:
365 Key Texts of the New Testament*
William E. Bowles

*Eight Stages of Christian Growth:
Human Development in Psycho-Spiritual Terms*
Philip A. Captain/foreword by Jerry Falwell

How to Pray: Discovering New Spiritual Growth Through Prayer
Barbara A. Gawle

Frustration: How Christians Can Deal with It
Frances Carroll

*How to Talk with God Every Day of the Year:
A Book of Devotions for Twelve Positive Months*
Frances Hunter

*God's Conditions for Prosperity:
How to Earn the Rewards of Christian Living*
Charles Hunter

*A Child of God: Activities for Teaching Spiritual Values
to Children of All Ages*
Peggy D. Jenkins

Prentice-Hall International, Inc., *London*
Prentice-Hall of Australia Pty. Limited, *Sydney*
Prentice-Hall Canada Inc., *Toronto*
Prentice-Hall Hispanoamericana, S.A., *Mexico*
Prentice-Hall of India Private Limited, *New Delhi*
Prentice-Hall of Japan, Inc., *Tokyo*
Prentice-Hall of Southeast Asia Pte. Ltd., *Singapore*
Whitehall Books Limited, *Wellington, New Zealand*
Editora Prentice-Hall do Brasil Ltda., *Rio de Janeiro*

Stephen J. Vaudrey
How to Win Your Family to Christ
A SPECTRUM BOOK
PRENTICE-HALL, Inc.,
Englewood Cliffs, N.J. 07632

Library of Congress Cataloging in Publication Data

Vaudrey, Stephen J.
    How to win your family to Christ.

    (Steeple books)
    "A Spectrum Book."
    Bibliography: p.
    Includes index.
    1. Evangelistic work.   2. Family—Religious life.
I. Title   II. Series.
BV3793.V38   1985   248'.5   84-22350
ISBN 0-13-441346-6
ISBN 0-13-441338-5 (pbk.)

To Karen and our children,
Becky, Bradley, and Wendy

© 1985 by Prentice-Hall, Inc., Englewood Cliffs, New Jersey 07632.
All rights reserved. No part of this book may be reproduced in any form
or by any means without permission in writing from the publisher.
A Spectrum Book. Printed in the United States of America.

10 9 8 7 6 5 4 3 2 1

Editorial/production supervision by Marilyn E. Beckford
Cover design by Hal Siegel
Manufacturing buyer: Frank Grieco

This book is available at a special discount when ordered in
bulk quantities. Contact Prentice-Hall, Inc., General Publishing Division,
Special Sales, Englewood Cliffs, N.J. 07632.

ISBN 0-13-441346-6

ISBN 0-13-441338-5 {PBK.}

CONTENTS

FOREWORD

Is there anything more heart-breaking than an unsaved family member, one who seemingly resists every effort at reconciliation with Christ?

We receive thousands and thousands of letters at Revivaltime Media Ministries. Many of them concern this very problem: "How can I win my father or mother or son or daughter or husband or wife to Christ?" The pull of the world system on some people is quite overwhelming. Our loved ones come into a bondage that seemingly all the love and persuasion in the world cannot break.

But there is hope! Tremendous hope! And my dear friend and fellow minister Stephen Vaudrey has been blessed with some profound insights in this area of common concern. I believe that the Holy Spirit has planted the seed for this book in Steve's heart, and you will be the beneficiary of his hard work and dedication in setting forth those divine principles.

You will not read standard clichés and tired bromides within these pages. This is an insightful and original commentary that will challenge you to "stir up the gift of God that is in you." And, by faith, I say that you will see salvation miracles in your household.

May this be the year in which everyone in your house is "covered by the blood." The need is urgent to win our family members, and I will ever be grateful to Steve for accepting the God-given burden to write this needed volume.

God bless you.

DAN BETZER

speaker, Revivaltime Media Ministries

PREFACE

"How can I help lead my family to a personal faith in Jesus Christ?" This book has been written to help you answer that question. Every Christian needs to know how to win his own family members to Christ, whether they are a parent, child, youth, single adult, grandparent, or other relative.

Although you are probably most familiar with the *direct* witnessing approach, your family can also be effectively reached with the gospel message through the *influence* of your everyday Christian life. In fact, in family evangelism efforts, a balance is needed between both the direct and indirect approaches.

There is also a need to understand the changes that have taken place in the composition of families. In the past, the traditional family—working father, homemaker mother, and children—was the predominant social unit. But today we must expand our concept of family to include those family groups having only one parent, older single adults, childless couples, families blended through divorce, and so on.

Whatever your family status, your ultimate goal is to share Christ in His glory and majesty and to allow the Holy Spirit to energize and excite you in your task of witnessing.

This book is presented in three sections. The objectives of Section One will be to review the concept of family evangelism, to discuss the proper climate for witnessing, to suggest a successful strategy, and to observe various approaches for winning specific family members to Christ.

Section Two offers a plan of attack for dealing with specific types of prospects you may encounter.

Section Three is a Scripture First Aid Kit to help you select just the right treatment for the spiritual and emotional scratches and bruises we all experience. This "kit" offers a "Band-Aid" approach to witnessing (meeting a felt need) that, used under the right circumstances, can have a profound effect on the one you wish to win to the Lord.

Although a book of this nature cannot, and need not, cover all soul-winning techniques and methods, the principles described will work in your family—because they are based on the Word of God. Such principles, although they focus on your family members, are not limited to those who reside at your address.

Keep this in mind: Your patience, understanding, and good relationships provide the *key*; God's presence in your life provides the *power*; and God's Word in your mind and heart provides the *assurance*—everything you need to lead your family to salvation.

We now begin Section One by reviewing the historical concept of family evangelism in both the Old and New Testaments and by identifying some obstacles you may face in your efforts to win your family to Christ.

This book was first published and distributed in booklet form by Revivaltime Media Ministries, the international broadcast outreach of the Assemblies of God. The demand from broadcast listeners, Bible study classes, and churches across the country has led to the preparation of this expanded version.

For his help in writing the original work, I am indebted to Larry Summers, who is an ordained minister and a family ministries consultant with the Assemblies of God Sunday School Department. Gratitude is also expressed to Debra King for her assistance in preparing the manuscript for this book and for her proofreading help during its production.

Scripture quotations marked (NIV) are from the Holy Bible, New International Version. Copyright © 1973, 1978, International Bible Society. Scripture quotations marked (NASB) are from the New American Standard Bible, © The Lockman Foundation 1960, 1962, 1963, 1968, 1971, 1972, 1973, 1975, 1977. The Living Bible is also quoted. Unless otherwise indicated, all other biblical references are from the King James Version.

I

THE CONCEPT
OF FAMILY EVANGELISM

Even in that beautiful paradise of Eden, God and Adam knew something was missing! So God made a woman. And from that time the context in which all human beings would live was changed forever. The family had begun.

It seems that God intended that we learn life's lessons best in family groups. From the very beginning God elected to work through families to bring truth to humanity. He could have selected angels or some other means to witness to His glory. When you stop and think about how God has purposely limited His awesome power, in working through the weaknesses and inadequacies of families, you cannot help but appreciate both the family and God more and more.

Let's take a moment and look at how God views our families.

The Old Testament reflects the Jewish understanding of the importance of family. The family served as the vehicle through which God's Word was passed from generation to generation.

Although sin entered the world and spoiled paradise, it did not spoil God's intention that mankind would live in fellowship with Him. Nor did it spoil God's intention that the family function as the primary means of preserving and communicating the truths of God's Word.

It is interesting that in God's original promise to Abraham, families would be blessed as a result of God's plan. ("In thee shall all families of the earth be blessed [Genesis 12:3].") Obviously, this blessing had to do with God's will that mankind should live in fellowship with Him.

The family, or household, continued to play a significant role in the unfolding of God's salvation plan. Family groups, kinship, and the tribe were the most important components of ancient Israel's social structure. The Hebrew word *mishpacha,* used in more than 95 percent of the Old Testament references to family or families, is a term we would interpret today as "extended family." It includes the whole circle of relatives, often including an entire tribe.

The religious commitment of the entire nation depended on its families' commitment to God. When the families of Israel followed God's will, the nation as a whole was blessed. When they did not, they suffered. That is why each household was commanded by God to honor and follow His leadership: "And ye shall rejoice before the Lord your God, ye, and your sons, and your daughters, and your menservants, and your maidservants, and the Levite that is within your gates [Deuteronomy 14:26]." "And thou shalt bestow that money . . . for whatsoever thy soul desireth: and thou shalt eat there before the Lord thy God, and thou shalt rejoice, thou, and thine household [Deuteronomy 14:26]."

When the Law was about to be given, God told Moses to call together the priests and all the elders of Israel. But He also gave specific instructions to gather together the *entire family* to hear, learn, and observe: "Gather the people together,. men, and women, and children, and thy stranger that is within thy gates, that they may hear, and that they may learn, and fear the Lord your God, and observe to do all the words of this law [Deuteronomy 31:12]."

The Old Testament considered the sum of all the families, clans, and tribes—the entire nation—as the "house of Israel" (2 Samuel 1:12). The New Testament continues the Old Testament concept of including larger groups in its meaning of "family." The most common term for family in the New Testament is the Greek word *oikos*. Like many Greek words it carries a basic meaning and can be expanded to include other meanings as well. *Oikos* has the basic meaning of "house" or "dwelling." Its broader meaning, however, is that of household or family. It is this broader meaning that is important for this study of family evangelism.

The apostolic church used the family, common kinships, and the community as means to spread the gospel. Listed below (emphasis mine) are some of the verses of Scripture that illustrate the importance of the family in the New Testament.

Return to *thine own house*, and show how great things God hath done unto thee. And he went his way, and published throughout the whole city how great things Jesus had done unto him [Luke 8:39].

And Jesus said unto him, This day is salvation come to *this house*, forasmuch as he also is a son of Abraham [Luke 19:9].

So the father knew that it was at the same hour, in the which Jesus said unto him, Thy son liveth: and himself believed, and *his whole house* [John 4:53].

. . . A devout man, and one that feared God with *all his house*, which gave much alms to the people, and prayed to God always [Acts 10:2].

And Cornelius waited for them, and had called together *his kinsmen* and near friends [Acts 10:24].

And when she was baptized, *and her household*, she besought us, saying, If ye have judged me to be faithful to the Lord, come into my house, and abide there. And she constrained us [Acts 16:15].

And they said, Believe in the Lord Jesus Christ, and thou shalt be saved, *and thy house* [Acts 16:31].

And I baptized also the *household* of Stephanas [1 Corinthians 1:16].

Now that we have looked briefly at the Old and New Testament concepts of the family, how do we apply them to the present?

A close study of human behavior indicates there are worldwide *units* of people or society. These include common kinships consisting of blood relations. This is what we often refer to as the traditional family. These groupings often include the extended family or blood relations such as cousins, grandparents, and Mom and Dad. The widening circle reaches to friends, neighbors, and those with common interests such as associates, co-workers, recreational acquaintances, and so forth. These social systems are not only representative of life in our country but are discernible throughout the world.

As we think about reaching our immediate family with the gospel we must also see that we are a part of a greater family, the whole family of mankind. Starting with our blood relations, we must also reach out to our closest neighbors, the paperboy, the gas station attendant, and ultimately around the world. Each day we must apply the principles God originally gave to the Jewish people to our family—immediate *and* extended—if we are to realize the benefits promised to them and to us. (See Deuteronomy 6.)

In ancient times, the Jews observed family worship through celebrations and commemorations. The whole family participated. When the children asked questions about these celebrations, the fathers would explain. (See Exodus 12:24–27.) It was through such observances that God-centered Israelite families passed their traditions, truths, history, and devotion from parent to child, generation after generation.

Although we do not observe these Hebrew ceremonies, we can still learn from them. Many of their values are profitable for us today. For example, when we observe family worship in our home, we gain a number of benefits. Here are some of the more obvious ones:

* ★ *Knowledge about the Bible.* Daily Bible reading and study produce a familiarity with God's Word that is attainable in no other way.
* ★ *Knowledge about God's will.* Studying the Scriptures gives the family a sense of God's ways. Forming a true concept of God in children is an important element in leading them to Christ.

* *Knowledge about prayer.* Families learn to trust God through praying and receiving answers from Him.
* *Knowledge about spiritual growth.* Children are taught, through family worship, to translate Biblical principles into everyday life.
* *Knowledge about the Church.* Families who worship together learn to appreciate the mutual support that exists between the fellowship of believers and the individual Christian.
* *Knowledge about family relationships.* When families worship together they open up avenues toward meaningful communication.

Religious education in the home and family was to be a fact of life for the Israelites. Parents were exhorted in Deuteronomy, Chapter 6, to apply God's commandments to everyday happenings and activities in the home. In short, it was to be a nurturing experience so that sons and daughters might grow spiritually, mentally, socially, and physically in a balanced way.

So it should be for families today.

How difficult will it be for you to lead your family to accept and worship Christ? Perhaps it will be an easy task. But more than likely, you will encounter some difficulties, both from within yourself and from outside forces.

One hindrance may be that of fear. If you are a new Christian, sharing your faith may be an unfamiliar venture. Or perhaps you have been saved for some time but have never been able to reach out to your family. In either case, fear is a common human reaction to any situation in which you sense the possibility of failure or rejection.

To combat the force of fear, you may use the great promise found in 2 Timothy 1:7: "For God hath not given us the spirit of fear; but of power, and of love, and of a sound mind." In the face of the fear of rejection, always recognize that fear is a hindering force coming from Satan and must be replaced by the greater powers of Christian love and discipline. Claim the promise of God, and reach out to your family through compassionate, unconditional love.

If your family members are like most people today, their priorities are not set on spiritual concerns. Today's secularized, depersonalized, rapid-paced life has caused many people to retreat into a shell and abandon the hope of ever finding meaningful relationships. There is a real need for awakening the family of God to the challenge of family evangelism.

Whatever your circumstances, you may be assured that the Spirit of God will help you share your faith with your family. You should recognize, however, that there is more than one way to lead your family to Christ. Some Christians make bold attempts to directly confront family and friends with the message of the gospel. This may be all right—provided the witnessing person is convinced that this is the best possible way to share his or her faith.

Others choose the indirect approach to witnessing by leading family members and friends to Christ through their *influence*. This method, of course, is a process that requires much patience and understanding, but it is often a very effective form of witnessing.

Probably the most effective strategy for sharing the message of Christ with others combines both methods—direct action and indirect influence. But whatever approach you choose, you can be sure that family soulwinning will be one of the most exciting, challenging, and rewarding tasks you will ever perform in this life.

CREATING THE CLIMATE FOR FAMILY EVANGELISM

Every backyard gardener knows how senseless it is to throw good seed onto soil hardened by the winter months. He knows the ground must first be prepared. It is the same with sowing the gospel. Like gardening, Christians must prepare the soil of the heart beforehand in order to reap a maximum harvest from the seed that is sown. Of course, God is the "Master Farmer" who makes plants grow, but a wise "gardener" will cooperate by casting the seed of the gospel onto soil that has been adequately prepared.

The effectiveness of family evangelism depends greatly on the proper climate and conditions within the home. A healthy spiritual climate (the relationships among family members) is of utmost importance.

A family whose spiritual resources are inadequate will naturally be hindered from becoming involved with others. When major unresolved conflicts exist between husband and wife, parents and children, or children and children, it is extremely difficult for the family to be effective and influential when dealing with others. A harmonious family relationship is essential for developing a climate for Christian faith.

There are four major avenues through which we reach our family. The first is *cultivating Christian values within the home*. A Christian lifestyle reflects the true commitment of a family to the lordship of Christ. The faith of even one person in the family will go a long way toward directing daily activities, influencing attitudes, and governing the use of resources for Christian values.

The abiding presence of the Holy Spirit within the believer gives a feeling of security even to unsaved family members. Christian love strengthens every fiber of family relationships. Most daily stresses, regardless of their nature, dissolve as the presence of the Holy Spirit works within the believing parent or other family member.

A second major avenue through which we can reach our families is to *recognize and affirm the vast human potential of each family member.* Scripture says, "And God blessed them, and God said unto them, Be fruitful, and multiply, and replenish the earth, and subdue it: and have dominion over the fish of the sea, and over the fowl of the air, and over every living thing that moveth upon the earth [Genesis 1:28]." What power that gives each one of us!

Created in God's image, each person has been granted a special uniqueness and individuality. It's important that you "see" this God-given potential in each member of your family, but it's just as important to let them *know* you see it. This is tremendously necessary for conditioning the soil and creating a climate for family evangelism. It's much easier, for example, to convince your son or daughter that God sees something worthwhile in him or her if the child is convinced that you do, too. So, don't forget—affirm personal potential!

Meeting your family's personal needs is another way of conditioning the soil and reaching your loved ones. Family members who starve for the vital elements of love, acceptance, and appreciation seldom are responsive to Christian teaching. It's just hard for them to get excited about such undemonstrated truth. A loving Savior can often be best demonstrated through the love and appreciation shown by a Christian family member. Let them see an example!

But don't stop there. God not only displays His love, He *tells* it. Each individual in your family needs to hear from you those important words, "I love you," and "I appreciate you."

Think of the most loving act you can imagine for each member of your family and plan to share it with each one. Make a list and write beside each name what you intend to say and do to meet that person's needs. Before long the entire family can be transformed from an emotionally starved condition to being filled with a living anticipation for the message of the gospel.

Accepting life's unfolding experiences, good and bad, is the fourth major way of creating the proper climate for effective family evangelism. Families who develop the will and disposition for Christian faith are those who lay aside resentment, jealousy, and selfishness and cultivate joyful zest for life and peaceful coexistence.

Even though you may feel that your family situation is one of hopeless stress and confusion, continue to trust in the plan of God. Faithfully trusting God's purposes may be difficult, especially under stressful family circumstances, but the encouragement of Hebrews 13:5–8 is reassuring: "Be content with such things as ye have: for he hath said, I will never leave thee, nor forsake thee. So that we may boldly say, The Lord is my helper, and I will not fear what man shall do unto me. Remember them which have the rule over you, who have spoken unto you the word of God: whose faith follow, considering the end of their conversation. Jesus Christ the same yesterday, and today, and forever."

Paul also reminds believers in Philippians 4:10–13 that contentment can be a part of Christian living each day. Families learn to trust God by experiencing contentment in all of life's events. Witnessing for Christ includes being content and at peace in the difficult phases of life as well as in the easier situations (see 2 Corinthians 12:10).

Recently, a middle-aged Christian lady shared a testimony of how she, as a teenaged girl, was forced by her mother to leave home. Fortunately, she was placed in a Christian foster home and introduced to Christ. Over the years she prayed every day for God to remove her bitterness and save her mother. However, every attempt to visit with her mother ended in heated arguments and bad feelings.

Then one night, many years later, she received a long-distance call from a sister informing her that their aging mother was desperately sick and not expected to live. Immediately, the Christian daughter began calling her friends and asking them to join her in fasting and prayer that her mother would be saved before dying.

Within hours she was at her mother's bedside, and the next few days were spent together in conversation. On one of those final days her mother reacted favorably to the Christian daughter's request to read the Bible to her. After reading the Scriptures, the daughter shared her lifelong desire that her mother would accept Christ before departing this world. Then she asked her mother if she would like to receive Christ. To the daughter's surprise, the aged mother nodded and received Jesus into her heart by praying the sinner's prayer.

It was then that the daughter heard from her mother's own lips words she did not remember ever hearing before: "Honey, I love you." A day later the mother passed away.

This true story is an inspiration to all of us who want to see every member of our family saved. Your family members may be resisting the gospel right now, but keep trusting, praying, and building a wholesome family climate. Sooner or later, you'll find your efforts worthwhile.

STRATEGIES FOR FAMILY EVANGELISM

In the first two chapters we discussed family evangelism in the light of the Old and New Testaments and in terms of the climate necessary for effectiveness. We now ask two questions: "Does family evangelism work in today's world?" and "Will it work in my family?"

To answer those questions, let's look at some recent research conducted by George Gallup and the Institute for American Church Growth.

Church Growth: America, the bimonthly magazine of the Institute for American Church Growth, carried an analysis of a recent Gallup poll that showed the following:

1. Levels of belief and religious practice remain high.
2. Interest in religion is growing sharply.
3. The evangelical movement is having an increasingly powerful impact on religious life in our world.

These findings let us know that a fertile field for evangelism exists all around us and especially within our families. Win Arn, the Institute's president, concludes, "There is a great receptivity to the gospel today that is unprecedented in the last 20 years."

A recent research program one year after Billy Graham's Seattle Crusade measured results that showed that the influence of family, friends, and relatives had a strong impact on effective evangelism follow-through. The research revealed that almost 83 percent of those who became members of a church as a result of the crusade did so because of the personal invitation of a friend or relative.

In bold contrast to the results of the Graham crusade were those of a nationwide telephone evangelism campaign conducted a few years ago. Follow-up surveys revealed that only 3 percent of those who said they accepted Christ "over the phone" were ever incorporated into a church.

These contrasting results demonstrate the problems often encountered when evangelism is impersonal and done between strangers. They show that an exclusively non-family approach to witnessing strains the concept of the New Testament, which emphasizes that disciples are more than verbal converts. Evangelism is most effective when it is personal and meaningful to both the one doing the witnessing and the one being witnessed to.

Other surveys and statistics consistently support the idea that family members sharing Christ within the family is the most effective means of fulfilling Christ's commission.

Now let's talk about strategy.

We've said that reaching your family members with a direct, verbal approach can be an effective method of evangelism. Linked with that is another important approach whereby we demonstrate the gospel message through our daily living. Both approaches are relevant and meaningful.

Keep in mind that some family members respond to the gospel almost immediately whereas others take much longer. Whatever time it takes and whatever approach you choose, always remain true to the goal of reaching every member of your family for Christ!

Here are some ideas for implementing the *indirect* approach strategy to evangelism:

Host a Bible Study or Christian Growth Group

You will want your family and guests to feel they are welcome and that fellowship and Bible study are primary goals of the meeting. Ask someone to lead the group for you and let your family serve as host. Invite several Christian friends or community members as well as an unsaved family. This will expose both your family and others to the gospel.

Invite Neighbors to a Cookout with Your Family and Some of Your Christian Friends

This will expose those you want to reach to wholesome Christian-related activities. This type of event will show your guests and family that Christians know how to laugh and enjoy life.

Open Your Home to Clubs and Other Groups

Groups for children, youth, or adults such as mission organizations, scouts, campus organizations, and business or professional clubs often need places to meet or would welcome a change of scenery. Invite an unsaved family to come or let their children participate.

Be a Good Neighbor

Show your family that you care about other families on the block. Be sensitive to what happens next door. Watch their home when they are away. Look for ways to get together.

New Neighbor Visitation

If your community is like most, there is a large turnover of families. Ask a family member to help you visit newcomers. Help them get acquainted with their neighbors and the new town. Be a spiritual "Welcome Wagon" by sharing information about your church and your faith.

Morning Coffees

Homemakers may be interested in visiting your home for refreshments, a brief Bible study, and a period of testimony and discussion. Family, neighbors, friends, and church acquaintances could be invited to attend.

Sports Time Out

Invite neighboring families into your home to watch a national sports event on television. Be sure to provide activities for those

family members who are not interested in that type of enter-
tainment. Plan a time of Christian sharing and fellowship for
the entire group.

The best ideas for you and your family will be the ones
you plan carefully. The goals of any of these projects are to
keep your faith alive, indirectly expose your family to the
gospel, and lovingly reach out to others in your community.

Family evangelism works. It worked in New Testament
times, and it works today.

WINNING THROUGH YOUR CHURCH

Before considering the specifics of winning individual family members to Christ, let's look at how you can become a dynamic witness *without* having any special skills or talent.

One of the best routes to effective Christian influence is to involve yourself in the outreach efforts of a soulwinning church. You don't have to "go it alone" in winning family and friends to the Lord; not when you can plug into your church's outreach ministry. It's the old concept of "many hands making light work." In this case, making *light* work—the light of the gospel.

No doubt you are familiar with that catchy little tune: "Reach out, reach out and touch someone." Every day the telephone company invites its customers to "call up and just say hi."

The first time I heard that ad it occurred to me that this little jingle could be a good theme song for church outreach. That's because outreach begins when people reach out and touch other people. Programs and plans for evangelism are important, but real evangelism often begins with a personal contact—when someone "calls up and just says hi."

Outreach really is a personal thing. Win Arn gave this startling result of his survey of 8,000 evangelical church members: "70 to 90 percent of those surveyed said the reason they came to Christ and their church was friends and relatives." Only "2 to 4 percent listed the church programs as the major factor."*

*Win Arn, "Four Ways You Can Help Your Church," *Pentecostal Evangel* (January 7, 1979).

Said Mr. Arn, "The fact is clear: church growth is largely related to present members influencing their friends and relatives."

In other words, evangelism often begins when someone inside the church reaches out and touches someone outside the church—someone he or she knows.

Whether or not you consider yourself "good" at witnessing, you can become a partner in outreach with your church. You can bring someone to Christ. All you have to be is willing to reach out.

Here is how you can reach out and touch someone in five simple steps.

Extend—to Meet a Need

You may not be able to relate great spiritual truths; you may not be able to preach a sermon. But you can show kindness; you can lend someone a helping hand. It's always easier for someone to take the hand of Jesus when your hand is reaching out.

Unconverted people are usually not interested in hearing a sermon, but they are always interested in having their needs met. When you extend yourself to help someone in need, you are relating your Christian testimony in a way that can be understood, accepted, and appreciated.

Jesus used this method to win people's hearts. He "went about doing good, and healing all that were oppressed [Acts 10:38]." In fact, He spent more of His time meeting people's needs than He did preaching. He demonstrated truth! They may not have understood everything He said, but they received Him when He reached out and touched them.

Ensure—with Love

After extending yourself and your resources to meet someone's need, this second step "reels 'em in." It brings him or her in for a closer look at the Jesus in your life, and ensures attention.

Love-filled action is Christian testimony on display. The persuasive power of demonstrated love often extends far beyond the receiving range of a spoken testimony. It reaches beyond the mind and penetrates the heart, allowing your prospect to experience the Christian message.

Then when the time does come for you to share your verbal testimony, he will be able to relate to God's love; he has already observed it in your life.

Enter—into Worship

When the one you wish to win to the Lord knows you are interested in his needs and that your love accepts him as he is, he just might accept your invitation to come to church—at least as a spectator.

Because "the natural man receiveth not the things of God," the worship service might make him a little nervous. That can be expected. But a good worship service can also give him an inner desire to become a part of the joy, peace, and love he senses in the atmosphere. Sometimes this contagious effect of a spiritually alive worship service can do more to win the heart of an unsaved person than a whole series of "hellfire and brimstone" sermons.

So don't wait for "special meetings"; invite your family member or friend to the worship service. He may be nothing more than a spectator at first; but what a thrill you'll experience when you watch him walk to the altar, give his heart to Christ, and then enter into true worship.

Encourage—Through Fellowship

Don't let the brand-new convert remain on the sidelines of spectatorship. Include him in your group. The intimate fellowship atmosphere of your men's or women's group, youth group, or Bible study circle will encourage the new Christian to share his thoughts and express himself. This is necessary for his spiritual development and integration into the church family.

Educate—in Truth

Be patient. Many old ways and habits will begin to fall away as the new Christian matures. He needs to learn about the things of God. This is where discipleship comes in, and the church will play a major role. But though he may attend the new convert's class and participate in other introductory courses offered by the church, he will continue to look to *you* for guidance. So continue to reach out to him! Help him to integrate into his life what he is learning.

Now, let's look into specific ways of winning a husband, wife, child, or parent to Christ.

WINNING YOUR HUSBAND

If your husband is unsaved and you want to win him to the Lord, you have a fortunate husband, for he is under a special spiritual covering.

The apostle Paul explained that "the unbelieving husband is sanctified by the [believing] wife [1 Corinthians 7:14]." This means your mate has a tremendous advantage over many other nonbelievers; he is exposed to the work of the Holy Spirit through your presence and influence!

Here are seven suggestions that can strengthen your testimony and help win your husband to Christ.

Remember, How You Say It Is as Important as What You Say

Your tone of voice, the look on your face, and your physical gestures may come across more forcefully than your words.

Public speakers are aware of this principle. In their book *Reaching From the Pulpit*, Dwight Stevenson and Charles Diehl wrote: "Every time a person stands to speak he communicates in two languages simultaneously. One is the language of the mind. The other is the language of the feelings. These two simultaneous communications . . . may and often do say exactly opposite things."

When this happens, the message of the feelings cancels out the message of the mind. This is why so many times a wife's words just don't get across to her husband—the feelings are speaking more loudly than the words.

So be careful what you communicate by your emotions.

Watch Your Timing

The effectiveness of your words is directly related to *when* they are spoken. Be sensitive to the Lord's leading.

God himself is a good example of timing. "When the time had fully come, God sent his Son . . . to redeem [Galatians 4:4, 5; NIV]." Not only does He do the right thing; He also does it at the right time. When He communicates to us He goes into action at the appropriate moment.

As you are sensitive to the Lord's leading, you will be amazed at how often the Holy Spirit will provide you with that "just right" opportunity for your spoken witness.

Learn the Art of Silence

Communicating a message at the right time also implies knowing when *not* to say it. A right message spoken at the wrong time can equal a *wrong* message.

Learn to "let it cool." This will take some discipline on your part, but postponing what you "have to say now" can help make your testimony more effective.

Learn to Really Listen

The apostle James said, "Take note of this: Everyone should be quick to listen, slow to speak, and slow to become angry [James 1:19, NIV]." The more common problem in witnessing is not in knowing how to talk, but in knowing how to listen. Too often a communication problem is really a traffic problem; two directions of traffic are trying to use the same one-way lane. How often have you heard only one part of a message, because instead of listening you were already thinking about your response?

Be an Example of Christian Living

The best instruction is often through example. Some time ago I tried to put one of those assemble-it-yourself toys together. The more I read the instruction sheet, the more confused I became. After about an hour of frustration I decided to check the "empty" box to see if I might have missed something. I had. Inside was a picture of how the completed toy should look. Suddenly it all made sense. Not only could I see the finished product; but the photo also showed where all the nuts, bolts, and washers would go. What a difference it made! I had an example, not just words.

Portraying a true Christian life is your best testimony. The Bible puts it this way: "You wives, be submissive to your own husbands so that if any of them are disobedient to the word they may be won without a word by the behavior of their wives, as they observe your chaste and respectful behavior [1 Peter 3:1,2; NASB]." The basic idea here is that without a lot of talking you can win your husband to Christ through your Christ-like behavior.

Several years ago my office received the following letter from a woman in Iowa. She wrote:

I had decided to divorce my husband because he was an alcoholic and our marriage was going nowhere fast. Coming from a broken home, I knew how much heartache a divorce can cause a child. I wanted to be sure Jim was entirely to blame for our trouble, so I prayed this prayer: "Lord, help me to be the best wife I can be, so that if I divorce Jim, I can be sure I'm not to blame for Cindy's not having her daddy with us anymore."

It was a selfish prayer, but the Lord answered it, and in a way I never expected. Jim started to look to the Lord, and he began to change. To make a long story short, Jim accepted Christ as his Savior. The Lord completely healed him of alcoholism, restored our marriage, and later called him to the ministry.

The scriptural principle had worked! Even though unintentional, Jim was "won without a word by the *behavior* of" his wife.

Let Your Husband Help in the Religious Upbringing of Your Children

Here is a way to actually get your husband involved in spiritual things—appeal diplomatically to his sense of responsibility as a good father.

No man wants to be a failure in this area. You can remind your husband that family Bible reading and family devotions will help give your children a solid foundation of moral values. Urge him to attend Sunday school and church with you "for the children's sake." Point out that in this way he will set a good example for his little boy who wants to grow up to be "just like Dad." This approach appeals to a man's ego. Many a husband has been won to Christ this way.

Never Give up!

This step is vitally important. It can't be stressed enough. Too many Christian wives have become discouraged because they haven't been able to see early results. Their efforts to set a godly example for their husbands seem to go unnoticed. Pretty soon they think, "Oh, what's the use? I've tried so hard to be the kind of Christian wife I should be, but it's not doing any good."

Don't make that mistake. It's only natural that you should want your husband to respond to your efforts. If he does, great; but if he doesn't, don't give up. Your real objective is not his immediate response but his ultimate salvation.

Nora Mort, of Springfield, Missouri, knows the rewards of not giving up. Her letter was a great encouragement to all of us at the Revivaltime office. She wrote:

> For a number of years I have sent a request to the Revivaltime World Prayermeeting for my husband's salvation. Praise the Lord, this year I do not need to. Last year in November we went to Florida for the winter, as is our custom. (He is 73; I am 68, and we are retired.) Shortly after Thanksgiving, he said he was going to church with me and was going to get saved. I guess I was shocked, to say the least, as I had almost given up hope. I had prayed for him for over 30 years. He went to the altar that morning and gave his heart to the Lord. How wonderful it is to have him go to church with me. I would like to say to anyone who has prayed for a loved one for years: Don't give up! God does answer prayer.

A short time later, Nora sent a second letter. "Since writing to you in October," said Nora, "my husband has gone to be with the Lord. We had gone to Florida for the winter and had only been there 3 weeks when my husband became very ill. He lived 5 days. I stood by his bedside only a few short hours before he died. He assured me everything was alright between him and the Lord. How thankful I am that he knew the Savior and that I have the assurance of seeing him again one day."

Yes, Christian persuasion is a process. Your love for your husband and your desire to see him saved should make you willing to forego the reward of immediate response. Let the Holy Spirit take the time He needs to work effectively in your husband's heart. If you will be patient and give Him that time, you, and the Lord, can win your husband to Christ.

WINNING YOUR WIFE

You can win your wife to the Lord! You can do it if you are willing to follow the instructions outlined in God's Word.

The Bible offers a set of guidelines that include God's provision, process, and procedure for winning an unsaved wife to Christ.

God's provision: "The unbelieving wife is sanctified by her husband [1 Corinthians 7:14]." This means your wife has a special exposure to the work of the Holy Spirit through your presence and influence. She is under the spiritual covering of your leadership. As the leader and head of your home, you have the opportunity to gently lead your mate to a saving knowledge of Jesus.

God's process: "That they may be won without a word by your behavior [1 Peter 3:1]." This verse is really directed to the Christian wife who wants to win her husband to the Lord, but it applies equally well to the husband's efforts to win his wife. One of the best ways to present the Christian message to your mate (or to anyone for that matter) is by your own Christian example—not your "preaching," but your behavior.

God's procedure: "You husbands, likewise, live with your wives in an understanding way, as with a weaker vessel, since she is a woman; and grant her honor as a fellow-heir of the grace of life, so that your prayers may not be hindered [1 Peter 3:7, NASB]." Memorize this verse! Deposit its message in your heart! It must become your attitude, your philosophy, your method of operation, as you seek to win your mate to Christ.

You see, your wife cannot be forced into salvation; she must be *won*. But in order to win her to Christ, you must first win *her*. You must deal with her gently; understand her, love her, accept her, honor her. Then as you follow these Biblical guidelines in your relationship with her, God will honor your efforts and prayers for her salvation.

Here are seven ways you can apply this Biblical formula.

Accept Her

Though it may be difficult to accept her non-Christian ways, it is vital that you let your wife know that you accept *her*. There's nothing more important to a wife than to be assured that she is accepted by the man she loves.

Be careful with your criticism. Don't criticize your wife's habits or apparel; she will take it personally. She will feel that you are criticizing *her*. Even though you don't mean it, she will interpret your remarks as being personally degrading, and that would certainly be a step in the wrong direction.

Let your words and actions show your wife you accept her. It is not enough to just assume your wife knows; you must say and do those things that will make it clear to her. Let her know she is *unconditionally* accepted—as a person, as a woman, as a wife. If you fail to get across the message that you accept her, you'll have a hard time convincing her that the Lord does.

Understand Her

Remember—your wife, saved or not, is a woman. Her needs, weaknesses, strengths, and desires are those of a woman. That's why 1 Peter 3:7 says, "Live with your wives in an *understanding* way, as with a weaker vessel, *since she is a woman.*"

The better you understand your wife, the more successful you will be in showing her how Christ can meet her needs. It's OK to tell her that "Christ is the answer," but unless you understand her *questions* (her frustrations, desires, etc.) the idea that Christ is the *answer* won't mean very much.

Honor Her

"Grant her honor as a fellow-heir of the grace of life [verse 7]."

Never give your wife a putdown because she's a woman. Recognize her as a "fellow-heir of the grace of life." This is not the voice of women's lib; it is the Word of God. You are a man; she is a woman. But you both are *human,* and this is the Biblical basis for equal rights.

Granted, differences should be recognized; but more important is the fact that both men and women are created to share equal honor as members of the human race—"fellow-heirs of the grace of life."

Honoring your wife must be more than theory; it must be practical. Take time to give her compliments! An unsaved wife may expect to receive "holier-than-thou" criticism from her Christian husband. As a result, she may build up defenses making his Christian testimony difficult.

But this won't be your problem if you praise her. Your well-timed and heartfelt compliments will keep your wife from feeling you think she is inferior. She needs to know you recognize the good qualities in her life—qualities that will become even better when she gives her heart to the Lord.

Love Her

She may not feel her need for Christ, but she deeply feels a need to be loved. This is your key to open her heart. Your demonstrated love can be a Christian testimony. It will reach beyond your wife's mind and penetrate her heart.

The husband is to love his wife as Christ loved the Church. (See Ephesians 5:25.) Someone has suggested that a husband can love like Christ in the following ways:

- ★ *Initiating love.* An indirect but effective way to witness to your wife of God's love is to take the initiative in expressing yours.

- ★ *Sacrificial love.* Christ died for you. Are you willing to suffer loss for the benefit of your wife?

- ★ *Lifting love.* Christ's love is uplifting. He *lifts* His church to becoming what He wants it to be. Similarly, as a Christian husband you should seek to bring out the very best qualities in your wife. As you do, your love can *lift* her to the path of life eternal.

- ★ *Nourishing love.* Christ's love nourishes the inner person. Is your wife fed in her soul by the love you show her?

- ★ *Enduring love.* Christ continually expresses His undying love to us. His love is not fickle. It does not bloom and fade with every change in our circumstances. Is the love you show your wife an enduring love?

Pray for Her

Spend more time talking to God about your wife than you do talking to your wife about God. Prayer does more than just change things; prayer changes *people*. It changes attitudes. You could spend your lifetime trying in vain to change your wife's mind. God can do it overnight! Keep God's attention on your wife. Keep praying for her!

Encourage Her

A little sign on a desk in my office says, "Accept me as I am so that I may learn what I can become." I can't think of better advice for a husband who is trying to bring his wife to the Lord. As you encourage your wife in her good points and understand her weak areas, not only will she become a better woman; she will become more open to *spiritual* encouragement.

Lead Her

Although your wife may show no desire for spiritual things, it is important that you assume your role as the spiritual leader of your home. Without coming on too strong or appearing pushy, gather your family daily for a time of devotions. Most wives want their children to turn out right. If you convince her that a family altar will benefit your children, she will be interested; and as she participates, she will be exposed to the gospel.

Here's another important area of spiritual leadership: take your children to Sunday school. Even if your wife won't go to church, she will soon be getting the gospel from the lips of the little ones she loves so much. Class papers and pictures that "I colored myself" will begin working on her heart. Many a wife has been drawn to Christ through her children.

These Biblical guidelines are proven ways to win a wife to the Lord. As you follow these instructions and allow the Holy Spirit to guide you, you may find someday that you are the husband of a "new" wife—a member of the bride of Christ.

WINNING YOUR CHILD

One of the greatest thrills of my life has been that of leading people to accept Jesus Christ as their personal Savior. Over the years I have had the privilege to work in many settings where individuals were given the opportunity to be saved. Indeed, these were rewarding times for me. But as a parent I know that the greatest thrill a Christian can have is to lead his own child to the Lord.

Children, by nature, have great faith. They are generally quite open to the message of the gospel. In fact, Jesus used a child to illustrate the quality of real faith, and implied that adults must put forth an effort to adopt childlike faith characteristics if they would be saved. That's why childhood conversions are so important.

When should a Christian parent introduce his or her child to the plan of salvation? While the age of readiness may vary from child to child, more conversions are recorded in the 7- to 11- year age bracket than at any other time. In fact, *research indicates that 85 percent of all conversions occur during that age span.* Of course, children often do accept Christ before age 7 and certainly after age 11, but within that age group they are most susceptible and reachable with the gospel.

Winning your child to Christ consists of much more than simply leading him in the sinner's prayer. Winning your child means exactly that—*winning* him. It means, among other things, that through the process of daily activities and relationships you have cultivated in the soil of his heart a desire and expectancy for the things of God.

A verse of Scripture often quoted with respect to winning a child to Christ is Proverbs 22:6—"Train up a child in the way he should go: and when he is old, he will not depart from it." Someone has offered this interesting paraphrase of that verse: "Create a taste for the Lord in your child when he is young, and when he is old nothing else will satisfy." The quality of Christian life your child will have depends to a large degree on the day-to-day process of creating in his life a taste for Christ—even before you "lead" him to Christ. It is important to understand that children tend to think of God in the same way they think of their dad and mom. That's why a good relationship between parent and child is essential. For that relationship becomes a touchstone for everything the child is taught about God. It becomes his frame of reference, his model. If he has loving, understanding, and comforting parents, he will perceive God in this way. But if the relationship produces fear, he will likely shrink back from the thought of God reaching out to him. The father figure is especially critical here. There is a close correlation between the child's perception of his earthly dad to his Heavenly Father.

Winning your child to Christ by helping develop a "taste for the Lord when he is young" begins with building a solid, understanding, loving, trusting atmosphere in the home, and this takes effort. It means spending time—*enough* time. Someone once said, "The training of children is a profession where we must know how to lose time in order to gain it." It is difficult to lead your child to Christ unless you are willing to spend the time to play with him, talk with him, discover him and let him discover you.

Times of talking and mutual discovery not only catalyzes an excellent relationship between parent and child, it fosters "just plain ol' happiness." And I can't think of anything that can produce this kind of happy relationship better than taking the time to have a good conversation with your child on his own level.

The bottom line is this: When a child feels free to talk with you about *anything*, he will feel free to talk with you about the things of the Lord.

The time will come (probably sometime after age 6) to *verbally* direct your child in asking Christ to come into his heart. When this happens, both the method and message must be simple and clear. As you explain the plan of salvation, avoid using difficult and confusing words. Be sure he understands each step he should take.

Here are the basic steps for coming to Christ:

1. You must realize you have done wrong. Romans 3:23 says (use your Bible as you read), "For all have sinned and come short of the glory of God."
2. You must want to change the way you have been living (Acts 3:19).
3. You must believe that Jesus Christ can help you (John 3:16).
4. You must ask God to forgive you for what you've done wrong (Romans 10:9).
5. You must realize that if you ask God to forgive you for the wrong you have done, He will do it (1 John 1:9).

The purpose of a personal verbal witness is not to coax or force a child to respond. Children are free moral agents capable of acting, thinking, and choosing for themselves. Their wills are often stubborn, self-directed, and under the control of a nature bent toward sin. Yet God intends for each child to be given freedom of choice. Parents are guardians over a child's will, but the decision to follow Christ must be made personally and independently by the child himself.

The parent must also be careful to provide checks and balances for a child's will while refraining from crushing, manipulating, or controlling it. Many have been unable to function in later life because parents used their own will to dominate their child. Even well-meaning Christians have tried to force the will of God upon their children, causing them to rebel later in life. It is important that a child be given the right to choose his own personal and spiritual destiny.

Some may wonder, "Isn't it possible that children will just grow into this? Can't they accept the Lord without actually knowing when?" Well . . . yes and no. *No*—a child cannot simply "grow" into salvation as if it were a part of some routine process. Salvation is a crisis experience when God breaks through the "natural" order of things and changes a life. Being saved requires that God effect a definite work of grace, justification, and regeneration in one's life. But, on the other hand, one could answer, yes. *Yes*—it is possible for a person to have saving faith in the Lord without knowing the precise moment he was saved. There are many Christians who admit, "Well, I really do not remember when I accepted Christ as my Savior, but I do know I was saved" (I am one of that group).

However, it is possible that this can produce haunting feelings of uncertainty. Without having been given the advantage of a specific time and place, a youngster may go along and never really be certain in his mind whether he has accepted Christ or not. *So help him make certain.* Give him the advantage of remembering a specific time and a specific place. Your child may not remember the exact day, but he will always be assured that he did, indeed, accept Jesus Christ as his personal Lord and Savior.

You may not be able to select the most "appropriate" time and place for your child to receive Christ, but whenever he indicates that desire, a close face-to-face, one-to-one encounter will be most effective. Put your arms around him and make sure he fully comprehends the steps he is about to take.

After he understands the plan and the steps to salvation, guide your child in a simple prayer asking God to forgive his sins. You may suggest that he pray after you, repeating the words you pray.

Allow him to continue praying on his own for a while, and when he is finished ask, "Do you believe Jesus has forgiven your sins?" If he feels this assurance then explain that certain things are expected of a person once he has accepted Christ.

Show your child that praying and accepting Christ is only the first step one takes in obeying Christ's command. The fulfilling Christian life includes reading God's Word each day, spending regular time in prayer, and sharing your faith with your friends.

The type of influence and encouragement you give will mean much to your child's spiritual growth. Begin praying together on a regular basis. Offer daily prayers to God about the salvation of other family members and your child's friends.

Regular church attendance is important too. Enroll your child in Sunday school and in those community activities that will enhance his spiritual life. And be sure to keep in close communication with what happens at school, church, and between him and his playmates.

After you have led your child to Christ, begin to create an awareness of the presence of the Holy Spirit in his life. And as you rely on that same presence to lead you into the paths of proper Christian parenting, the Lord will help you to train your child in the way he should go, so that "when he is old, he will not depart from it [Proverbs 22:6]."

WINNING YOUR TEEN

"Our youth today now love luxury. They have bad manners, contempt for authority, disrespect for older people. Children now days are tyrants. They no longer rise when their elders enter the room. They contradict their parents, chatter before company, gobble their food, tyrannize their teachers."

The descriptive comment about typical youth behavior seems appropriate for today, when in fact, the statement was made by Socrates in the fifth century B.C.! It would seem that the tumultous time of youth is nothing new under the sun.

Guiding young people through their challenging teen years results in some great times and some bad times. However, these can also be some of the most rewarding years of your life as a parent even though the problems seem to get more complicated with each birthday that passes. Whatever the circumstances may be tomorrow, we need the constant awareness of God's wisdom and the constant assurance of His answers to our prayers for our children.

The word adolescence is derived from the Latin verb *adolescere*, meaning "to grow up" or "to grow into maturity." Several general definitions may be given for this exciting but frustrating stage of life. *Sociologically*, adolescence is the transition period from dependent childhood to self-sufficient adulthood. *Psychologically*, it is a transitional state in which new adjustments have to be made, namely, those that distinguish child behavior from adult behavior. *Chronologically*, it is the period from age 12 or 13 to the early 20s with wide individual and cultural variations.

The reason for stating these facts is to underscore the need for understanding our youth before we can effectively approach them with the gospel.

Two primary factors in the life-cycle development of youth should be considered. One factor relates to the pressures he feels from his peer groups or associates. As he seeks to establish some form of autonomy from his parents he may go to extremes in following the values, mores, and social sanctions of individuals outside the family circle. A parent who fails to understand this phenomenon will be distraught.

The other major factor in understanding youth relates to recognizing the need to identify with a meaningful cause or task. As a young person attempts to find his own values at his own level, he finds he must distinguish between his parents' and peers' opinions of him and what he perceives to be true about himself. A personal relationship with Christ and the challenge of Christ-like living could bring great meaning to this important phase of development.

With these facts in mind, we ask the question, "How do we most effectively reach our older child with the gospel of Christ?"

One thing is for sure: never approach older children or young adults in a preachy, judgmental fashion. Since they are sensitive to any authority figure, expecially parents, you will want to avoid probing, prying, or forcing any issue upon them. That is not to say a parent is to compromise morality or Biblical principles; you can hold to basic principles and at the same time avoid a negative, demeaning attitude.

What is often very difficult, yet most effective over the long term, is to establish a mutually open, trusting relationship with your teen and maintain a state of constant communication.

A prerequisite for establishing good communication with youth is effective listening. Not just hearing, but *listening*. There is a difference. Hearing is basically to gain content or information for your own purposes. Listening is caring for and being empathetic toward another person. Hearing means that you are concerned about what is going on inside of you during the conversation. Listening means you are trying to understand the feelings of the other person with his interest at heart.

There are at least three elements of effective listening to young people: (1) When your young person is talking to you, do not be thinking about what you are going to say after he stops. Concentrate on what is currently being said. (2) Completely accept, without judgment, what is being said and how it is said. Otherwise, you may fail to hear the message if you do not happen to like the tone of voice or the words used. Acceptance does not mean you have to agree with the content of what is said; rather, it means that you understand that your youth is saying something he feels. (3) Be able to repeat what has been said and what you thought was felt. Real listening requires an obvious interest in the youth's feelings and opinions and an attempt to understand them from his perspective.

Another part of listening is called "focused attention." Focused attention is giving your child full, undivided attention in such a way that he feels without a doubt that he is completely loved; that he is valuable enough in his own right to warrant his parent's undistracted attention, appreciation, and uncompromising regard. In short, focused attention makes your youth feel he is, in his parent's eyes, the most important person in the world.

Trying to spread effective listening and focused attention among several very alive and involved teens can be a great challenge. Different children make different demands, and it is easy to concentrate on one at the expense of the others. It is important in sharing Christ, and in the overall family atmosphere, to balance times of focused attention and listening among all family members.

In order to register a high level of influence on your young people (and the rest of your family), an atmosphere of honesty and truthfulness must prevail in the home. Ephesians 4:15 says, "But speaking the truth in love . . ."

Parents must exhibit the characteristics of honesty and integrity at all times. All parents are tempted, on occasion, to sidestep painful issues by manipulating their children. But children and youth are very seldom fooled when parents coerce them into conformity against their will. This type of parental behavior destroys the effectiveness of the Christian witness and presents an improper model before young people.

At times, young people will take advantage of their parents by altering the facts to protect themselves from the full impact of their misbehavior or wrongdoing. This must not be allowed to happen repeatedly and should be dealt with compassionately but firmly.

It's important to *think* before reacting to your teenager. Trying to remember how you felt about school, friends, dating, etc., when you were that age will allow you to avoid making unnecessary and unreasonable requirements, conditions that your children may not be able to meet.

To conclude our discussion of how to reach youth with the gospel, I want to encourage parents to always strive toward understanding. Both parents and youth need to see the world from each other's point of view. If parents model this attitude, young people will reciprocate.

Seeing another person's point of view may require a person to give up his own ideas *long enough to move mentally to the position of the other person.* The goal must be to understand! If our youth know that we understand or that we are at least attempting to understand them to the best of our ability, they will be more open to our testimony. An understanding attitude has been enough to cause a good number of young people to accept the Savior of their parents as their own.

WINNING YOUR PARENTS

How can you win your parents to Christ? Every Christian child or young person will admit that winning parents is no easy task, especially in view of some of the past problems in parent-child relationships. However, the first place a child should share his personal testimony should be in his own home!

The first step is to inform your parents in a personal, meaningful way about the circumstance prior to and during your conversion. Be sure to explain the inner, personal feelings, as well as the outward events that took place. Ask your parents to support you in your new decision.

During the course of your personal witness of faith, lead your parents to understand that a totally different lifestyle is expected of you as a Christian.

A good way to begin sharing your Christian faith is by asking your parents' forgiveness for past mistakes and behavior that have damaged vital family relationships. Be prepared to forgive other family members and your parents of hurts they may have inflicted upon you in the past. Let them know that, just as Christ forgave you, they have been unconditionally pardoned for all past mistakes.

Your most important method of reaching your parents for Christ comes through building bridges of reconciliation. Broken relationships hinder the movement of the Spirit of God within our lives and our family's life. They neutralize our witness and its importance. Broken relationships shut off the flow of love to all our world. If you would make a list of all the dark, sad, and unhappy times in your life, you would find that the vast majority of those times were created by strained or broken relationships. Then, if you would list all the warm, wonderful times of joy, and happiness, you would find that right relationships were the key. Right relationships with your parents must be at the center of your Christian testimony.

If your parents are not sympathetic to the gospel at the time of your conversion, you will need to select a strategy for *long-range* influence. Don't be discouraged if they aren't open at first. In time they will change their attitude if you pray and live the Christian life before them. They are watching your life every day and will see the changes that take place. Don't think they won't notice!

Practicing Christian disciplines each day will improve your relationship and provide a sure witness of Christian faith. A *discipline* is just what the word implies: a means through which we condition ourselves physically, socially, mentally, and spiritually on a consistent basis to accept the lordship of Christ in our lives. *Christian disciplines are intended to bring about change in our own lives and, at the same time, show our family members that our decision for Christ was serious.*

Reading the Word of God daily will lead you to understand the guiding principles of the Christian faith. While you read, allow the Holy Spirit to illuminate the truths in the Scriptures, and then apply them to your own experiences. Systematically read the entire Bible, beginning with the Gospel of John. Your family will know you've been spending time studying the Word of God because it will show. It will be displayed in your behavior.

Daily prayer is another discipline which will keep your faith strong in the face of temporary setbacks and obstacles. In Romans 8:26 the Holy Spirit is described by Christ as an indwelling intercessor who will help you pray. As you pray, form a mental image of your family while you ask the Holy Spirit to give you wisdom in leading them into the Christian faith. The process of intercession will work as we regularly take advantage of God's power and wisdom.

Combined, these disciplines are often called personal devotions. You can pray and read your Bible at separate times; but, try to couple these activities together, using a daily devotional guide or some other helpful piece of Christian literature.

Another way to influence and win your parents is to select wholesome Christian books, periodicals, and study materials for daily reading. You will be greatly affected by what you read and will be encouraged in your attempts to witness and win your parents and family members.

Regular association with the body of Christ through friendships and church attendance will help you with your Christian life and witness. Introduce your Christian friends to your mom and dad. Ask your friends to pray with you about your parents accepting Christ. Ask your Sunday school class members and other church friends to pray with you too. Ask your pastor to visit your home, meet your folks, and pray with you about your family's spiritual needs. Explore every means of support available through the body of Christ.

Contribute regularly and consistently to the ministry of the local church through Christian activities and financial support. Your church needs you, and you need the church. Sacrificial giving will strengthen your relationship and continue to discipline your will to conform to God's commandments.

Remember, love is meeting needs. God wants to meet even the deepest needs of your parents through you. You can see this happen first by loving the Lord God with all your heart, soul, and mind. How do we love God? When we love our parents in Jesus' name, we are loving God. When those who are precious to Jesus become precious to you, you are loving God with all your heart, soul, and mind. You are not really loving Jesus until you become a channel of His love in meeting needs. Through your love, God can use you to reveal himself to your parents.

There will be times when your parents may be especially receptive to the gospel. Certain events can have a direct affect on a person's responsiveness; events such as the death of a family member, personal injury or illness, change in health, mortgage loans, trouble at work, holiday seasons, and special family occasions. As you are sensitive to your parents' feelings during such times, they may become more interested in your testimony.

Just as the New Testament pattern of witnessing began in the Book of Acts through relationships that had already been established, so we must build and nurture vital relationships with parents and family members. A good relationship is the track your testimony runs on to reach your parents, and as love moves through that relationship, your parents' deepest longings will be met and your testimony will be strengthened.

WINNING THROUGH WEAKNESS

Let's take a break and shift our attention from the person you want to win to Christ to the person who will be doing the winning. You. The *winner.*

I think it is important to focus on *you* at this point, because if we don't, it's certain that the devil will. For Satan, you know, is as interested in keeping you from winning your family members to Christ as you are in winning them.

The most effective weapon Satan has to keep you from being a soul "winner" is to somehow make you believe you are a *loser.* That fits his style. His offensive has little to do with conventional warfare; his method of operation is the "personal affront front."

The apostle Paul explained it this way: "For we wrestle not against flesh and blood, but against principalities, against powers, against the rulers of the darkness of this world, against spiritual wickedness in high places [Ephesians 6:12]." In other words, Satan's efforts against your efforts cannot be countered with a physical defensive. The battleground is the mind and the spirit.

How do you fight such a battle? Paul gave us the key to that too. "For the weapons of our warfare are not carnal [fleshly], but mighty through God to the pulling down of strongholds; casting down imaginations, and every high thing that exalteth itself against the knowledge of God, and bringing into captivity every thought to the obedience of Christ [2 Corinthians 10:4, 5]."

From a mental and spiritual battleground Satan launches his most destructive offensive against your soulwinning efforts.

It is from this same battleground that you must mobilize your defense, *"casting down imaginations . . . and bringing into captivity every thought to the obedience of Christ."* Read that again. That is the key!

You see, if Satan can get you to imagine that you are a loser, he can keep you from ever becoming a soul *winner.* And you may be certain of it—he will exploit your weaknesses. He will accuse you. He will convince you, if he can, that you are worthless. And he knows that if he can do this, he will likely win in his efforts to paralyze your usefulness to the kingdom of God.

What you must realize is that the devil is in the home destruction business. But God is in the home construction business. The Lord will build you up so you can be useful to Him; Satan will try to destroy your strengths by reminding you of your weaknesses. But, with your cooperation, God will help you to win—*through* your weakness!

When I was in the third grade, I painted a picture of a bird. It was a gray bird, perched in the branches of a brown tree against a clear, blue sky. I could hardly believe the teacher when she told me that my picture had been selected to be entered in the art show. It was a city-wide exhibit representing the best artwork from each of the city's grade schools.

I was shocked! *How could my picture have been selected?* I wondered. Art was my worst subject. Curious, I hurried down to the exhibition building. Among the third grade entries I spotted my picture. Yes, there it was. My picture! But it was upside down!

My bird was a fish! A gray fish swimming through brown seaweed in clear, blue water. The picture I had made an effort to paint was probably the worst in the class—at least I thought it was—but the teacher had inadvertently turned it upside down and made my painting into a *winner.*

From that childhood experience I learned a valuable lesson: *There is winning potential in personal weakness.*

The apostle recognized this principle when he said: "Therefore I take pleasure in infirmities, in reproaches, in necessities, in persecutions, in distress for Christ's sake: for when I am weak, then am I strong [2 Corinthians 12:10]."

Paul knew the value of his weaknesses. They did not hinder him from doing the Lord's work. He was aware that God could use him—weaknesses and all—as a channel of divine strength.

Here are some suggestions that may help you as you allow the Lord to turn your weaknesses into a channel of strength.

Acknowledge Your Weaknesses

Be specific! Make a list of those areas in which you feel the need to be more effective.

Perhaps you feel weak in the area of your Christian witness. You know you should be witnessing, but you're not much of a talker. Or you'd like to have more friends at school, but you've always been somewhat shy. Or maybe you want to be a better mother, but you're a high-strung person and always end up yelling at the kids. Write it down.

Making an inventory of your weaknesses will accomplish three things. It will cause you to define the area of your need; it will enable you to be specific when praying about your need;

and it will allow you to turn an overall depressed feeling into a target for your faith.

One of the real problems of personal weakness is that it often does double duty. Instead of confining the particular weakness to what it really is, we often allow it to spill over into other areas. The cake flops, for example, and you say, "I'm a terrible cook; *I can't do anything right.*" Generalizing your weakness plants negative seeds that can actually weaken your strengths.

Concentrate on Your Strengths

After you acknowledge your weaknesses, don't focus on them. Instead, concentrate on your present abilities and insights—those things you can do. Never spend your energy on preoccupation with the things you "can't" do.

The Bible says to put your abilities to use—to invest them. When a person makes a financial investment, it draws interest; over a period of time the initial investment is increased. It's the same way with the ability God has given you. When you put it to work, it will grow.

Don't grow your weaknesses; grow your strengths!

Accept the Truth; Reject the Lie

As we have mentioned, Satan is a master of psychological warfare. His most effective weapon is the discouraging lie. He is an expert in smudging the real issues with vague and confusing suggestions.

After obscuring the facts, this enemy will attempt to manipulate your emotions. He will try to cloud your reasoning with baseless doubts about your ability and personality.

In his personal attack, the devil will try to get you to believe some of his famous lies, such as, "You're no good. You're a blah person. You're no help to your family. No one could ever love you. You don't have a speck of creativity." Recognize any of these? They're Satan's tactics designed to give you a negative attitude that will only weaken you further. He wants to destroy you, and your Christian influence.

But God deals with truth! He works in the area of fact and possibility. Ephesians 3:20 says, He "is able to do exceeding abundantly above all that we ask or think, according to the power that worketh in us." God is able to take those qualities already in you and develop them to a degree you never thought possible. This is the Biblical side of positive thinking.

It comes down to one simple question: Whom are you going to believe? Will you believe Satan, whose intention is to destroy you? Or will you believe the Lord Jesus Christ, who wants to strengthen you?

Never Accept the Verdict
of a Depressed Moment

Obtaining a fair verdict is the object of a court trial. But where evidence has been suppressed, such a verdict is impossible.

Whenever you make a critical decision during a moment of depression, you risk doing so without examining the facts properly. You may be suppressing evidence that is in your favor. When this happens, you become the victim of your own unfair trial. So whenever you become discouraged, a "motion to recess" is in order. Delay your decision until you can be more objective. Then, in a clearer light, your verdict will probably be a different one—and a better one.

Remember—Your Greatest Strength Can Be a Resolved Weakness

Just about anyone can minister their strengths to the needs of others, but it's often more effective to share strength through the weakness that God has helped you through. To be able to say, for example, "I know what you're going through; I've been through it too," can really touch someone's heart. And then to be able to say, "But God has helped me to get over my negative feelings, and He can do the same for you"—that's ministry! That's strength through weakness—weakness you and the Lord have overcome.

Submit Yourself to God's Creativity

God is the author of all creativity. His Spirit moved over the waters when the earth was without form and void. He created order out of chaos then, and He can do the same in your life today.

As an Artist, He can create significance and beauty out of the indiscriminate marks life has brushed across your "canvas."

As a Poet, He can create a lovely flow from a life that doesn't rhyme.

As a Musician He can take the circumstances of your life, arrange them to work together in harmony, and place a song of joy in your heart.

I watched little 4-year-old Tommy as he prepared for his new adventure. It was his very first jigsaw puzzle, and he was eager to get started. With a studious expression he carefully evaluated the situation to determine which part of the eight-piece puzzle he should begin with. A little while earlier he had watched some older kids putting a puzzle together, and now he was ready.

First piece selected, Tommy made several unsuccessful attempts to locate its proper place in the vacant area. Setting that piece aside, he selected another. Same results. He selected a third piece. Same thing. Nothing would fit!

Tommy's exasperation was beginning to show, and I was curious to see how he would handle it. But I certainly wasn't prepared for what happened next. Taking the three problem pieces in hand, Tommy got up from the floor, walked across the room, and casually tossed them into the wastebasket. "Don't need those," he muttered; "they're the wrong ones."

Suppressing a laugh, I suggested that Tommy and I go back and work on the puzzle together. Under my guidance the remaining five pieces found their proper places on the board. I turned to Tommy. "There," I said, "the *right* pieces are in place."

Without saying a word, Tommy went to the wastebasket, retrieved the three discarded pieces, and, without further help from me, completed the puzzle.

"Now," he said in a matter-of-fact way, "the picture is finished."

This little boy learned a lesson about how a puzzle works.

But more important, there is a lesson here about how life works, too. How unfortunate that some adults never learn such a lesson.

To many people, life is a puzzle that doesn't fit together. All the pieces are the wrong ones. The frustrations don't fit. The conflicts don't fit. Family problems don't fit. The pain doesn't fit.

These folks find it difficult to see how these "odd-shaped" pieces of life could possibly come together to form anything of beauty and purpose. They never really comprehend the promise of Romans 8:28 that "all things work together for good to them that love God." Consequently they reject some of the precious and vital pieces of God's plan for their lives. Life, to them, is not much more than confusing parts of a puzzle that sadly remains an unfinished picture.

There's more to the picture of your life than what you see. You may feel your efforts are worthless, but God sees the whole picture. And He looks at it from different angles. Sometimes there may be a piece missing; but sometimes all He needs to do is to turn your "picture" upside down (or right side up) to make it a winner.

WHAT SHALL I DO
IN THE MEANTIME?

"While I agonize over their fate, I also have a deep seated peace because God does all things well. I have committed them to God with a clear conscience, and continually pray on their behalf."—S. Robert Maddox.

What happens when nothing is happening? What goes on behind the scenes while you are praying and nothing seems to get off dead center with your witnessing efforts? Probably plenty. Most likely, God has some "wheels" in motion you know nothing about. Just be sure you don't do anything that would upset His plans and timing. It won't be easy, but your task is to simply be faithful, prayerful, and committed.

That applies no matter how skillful you might be at witnessing. Even ministers and full-time Christian workers are often among those whose family members are unresponsive to their testimony.

Reverend S. Robert Maddox is an example. The pastor of a congregation in Minnesota, Reverend Maddox often wonders why he is the only one in his whole family serving the Lord. Mr. Maddox has given permission to include in this book his account of what he is doing *in the meantime* while waiting for his family to turn to Christ:

A railroad engineer's son raised without religious training, why was I called into the ministry? What a shock it was to my family.

Why, even now since I have entered the ministry, don't other members of my family accept Jesus as their Savior?

It seems they are getting colder, rather than warmer toward the gospel.

I never pressured them to accept my beliefs. I was careful not to say or do anything to cause them to be turned off toward spiritual truths. I invited them to the many special meetings at the church, but they never came. I have prayed for them for the past 16 years, but nothing visible is happening.

Why was I so receptive to salvation, but they are not? I am of the same flesh and blood. I had the same upbringing. I come from the same heritage, yet they care nothing about God while my whole world revolves around Him.

It is hard to accept that if Jesus were to come today, my family would not be joining me in heaven. Still the Scriptures tell me to pray for His soon return—a difficult task when one's family is not saved!

Some friends tell me to claim their salvation. "Stand on the promise of the Philippian jailer and believe for them," they say (Acts 16:31). From reading the whole story, however, I discover that I am better off pleading to God for mercy on their behalf. I can't convict my family of sin; only the Holy Spirit can. I can't save them; only Jesus can. I can't claim their salvation for them; each person must decide for himself.

What then can I do that I haven't already done? I am where God wants me to be, but I live 1,600 miles away from their home. How can I witness to them from this distance?

Each day I agonize over the fate of my family. It is another part of life over which I have no control. When they accept Jesus, it will be by His power and grace. If they were to continue to reject Him, it would be of their choosing. I'm in the middle, feeling the burden but having no power to act.

I have been in this position for some time, and I have learned some things about trying to bring salvation to one's family.

First, *I cannot save them.* No matter how much I would like to, I cannot pray their prayer of repentance and faith for them. At the same time, I shouldn't carry any feeling of guilt for their indifference. I have done what God has led me to do, and I must not blame myself if they should choose against Him for eternity.

Second, *I must live a real and consistent Christian life before my family.* They don't see me as a minister, or even as a Christian; they see me as their son and their brother. No matter what they envision me as being, I must act like a child of God.

My way of life is confusing to them. How can things perfectly acceptable in my upbringing now be totally unacceptable in my children's upbringing? I am not acting superior, yet I will not live any less for Jesus in their presence. I must behave as a Christian should at all times.

One family member once said that I must have raised myself. No, my folks raised me, and Jesus refined me. I am who I now am in Christ Jesus. So I walk in His light and trust God that they will sense my genuineness.

Third, *I must resign myself to the possibility that I may not lead them to Christ but that they may become jewels in someone else's crown.* Where my influence may have diminished as a prophet rejected at home, others may find doorways wide open to share the gospel.

God has many more witnesses for my family than I may realize. He has the keys that can open those seemingly impenetrable hearts. I hope I can be there to see them get saved; but what is more important—their salvation or my leading them to salvation?

Now some may ask, "Why is this even an issue?" Because many of us are very possessive of our families; if we can't lead them to the Lord, we don't think anyone else will either. We need to clear the way and completely commit them to the Lord so that salvation may come in whatever way it can.

Finally, *I will never give up praying for my family.* There may not be any visible change, but prayer does on the inside what eventually emerges on the outside. They may be feeling the convicting power of God and not be showing it. Visible or not, something is happening because of prayer.

Continued prayer is my affirming to God that I still trust Him to work out their salvation. Prayer is my faith in action. Prayer is pronouncing to God that I haven't given up. I will continue to pray until I see the result.

I can pray for them with confidence and still pray for Christ's return. Both are in God's timetable, and He can bring them both to pass.

Though it hurts to see my family not experiencing God's blessings, I find comfort in knowing that if God can bring salvation to me, then He can bring it to them. My own salvation testifies that their salvation is not impossible.

While I agonize over their fate, I also have a deep-seated peace because God does all things well. I have committed them to God with a clear conscience, and I continually pray on their behalf. By His grace, someday I will see my family join me in His kingdom.

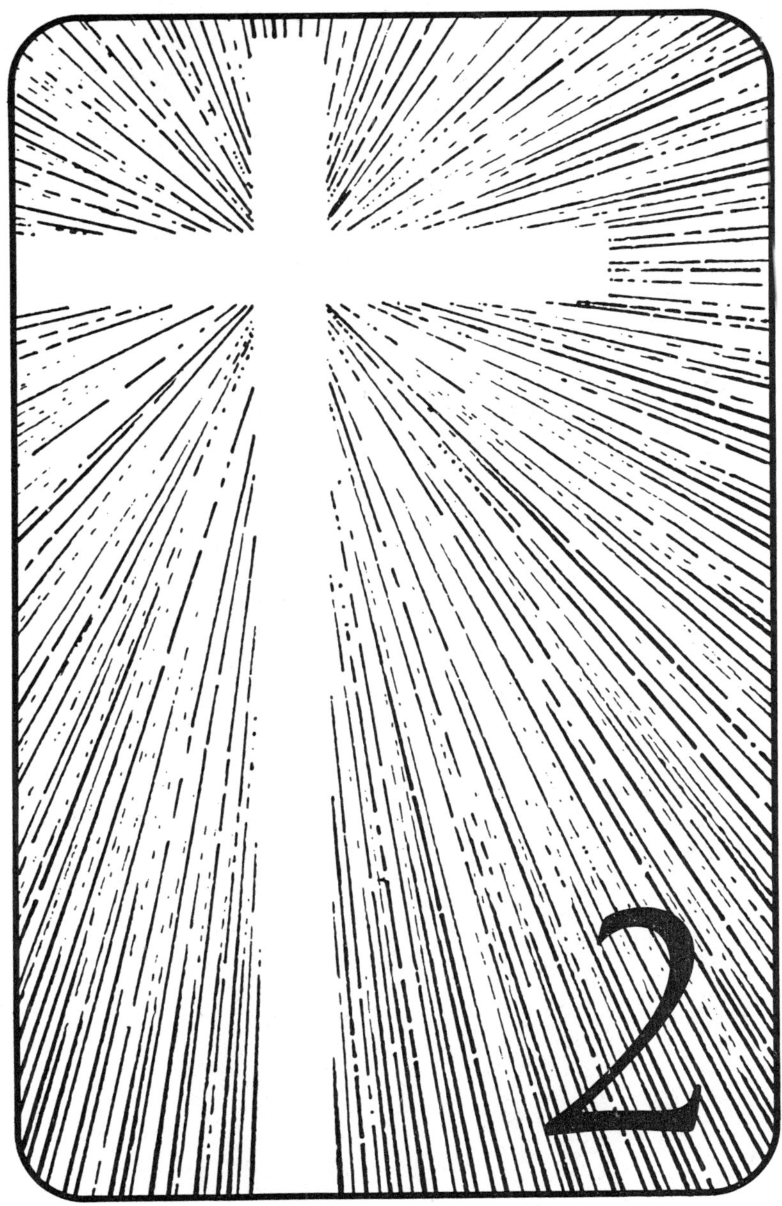

INTRODUCTION

To help you lead others to Christ—your relatives, friends, co-workers, etc.—this section will present the techniques of dealing with *types* of "prospects." We will examine several categories of individuals and discuss possible methods of dealing with each. However, as you read this section please remember that soulwinning is usually a *process*, and that technique can never take the place of a living witness and proper relationships.

While the techniques discussed in this section will apply mainly to those you witness to outside your own home, they should provide additional insight in dealing with members of your household as well.

The first type of prospect we will discuss is the one who is ready to receive the Lord as his Savior. He is the *seeker*. His heart has already been prepared through the seed sown by others, and now he is ready to be led to salvation.

Other types we will discuss are the *self-righteous* and the *procrastinator*. These will be more difficult to deal with.

Another type, the *fearful* person, may be afraid he's too great a sinner to be saved or that he may not be able to "hold out" as a Christian. Or, there are those who are fearful they may have committed the unpardonable sin. This particular fear is very real, very terrifying, and one that we will discuss in depth.

Keep in mind that this section is not offered as some sort of shortcut to "instant witnessing." It is presented as background material to help you in the *process* of winning your family and others to Christ.

WINNING THE SEEKER

This person is relatively easy to lead to the Lord. This one is ready and needs very little or no convincing. He already knows he is a sinner and in need of salvation. The Holy Spirit has been dealing with his heart, and he is anxious for you to show him how to be saved. (Wouldn't it be great if everyone you witnessed to were like this?)

Here are some suggested steps for dealing with the *seeker*.

Show Him Jesus Christ as the "Bill Payer"

Often, such an individual has been trying to get rid of his sins through his own efforts. He has wept and prayed time after time. Over and over again he has made commitments to be better, but his efforts have been to no avail.

Show this person that Christ has already "picked up the tab." He has already paid the bill through His death on Calvary. That was enough to completely cancel all his sins. "Let him that is athirst come. And whosoever will, let him take the water of life freely [Revelation 22:17]." "All we like sheep have gone astray; we have turned every one to his own way; and the LORD hath laid on him the iniquity of us all [Isaiah 53:6; see also John 5:24 and 1 Peter 2:24]."

Show Him How He Can Receive
This "Paid-For" Salvation

Salvation is received through Christ by repentance, a turning away from sin (Luke 13:3; Acts 2:38); confession (Romans

10:9); and appropriating faith (John 3:16; Acts 10:43, 16:31; Romans 10:9).

"If thou shalt confess with thy mouth the Lord Jesus, and shalt believe in thine heart that God hath raised him from the dead, thou shalt be saved [Romans 10:9]."

Show the Seeker That Christ
Has Risen from the Dead

Christ's resurrection means that the believer has been *justified*—"just-if-I'd" never sinned. (See Romans 4:25). To be justified means that God has erased the sinful past and that the believer now has a new standing with God (Isaiah 44:22). He is now actually called the friend of God (James 2:23).

Show Him That the Resurrected Christ
Is Now in Heaven Interceding for Him

"It is Christ that died, yea rather, that is risen again, who is even at the right hand of God, who also maketh intercession for us [Romans 8:34]." This is our guarantee that God the Father accepts those who come to Him through Christ.

Show Him That He Can Be Assured
of His Salvation

Make it clear to the one who has accepted Christ as Savior that he must not rely on his feelings as an indicator of his standing in the Lord. He must rest his faith in the *fact* of God's Word that he has been accepted through Christ, that he has been forgiven, that his sins have been washed away, and that he is a new creation in Christ. "If any man be in Christ, he is a new creature: old things are passed away; behold, all things are become new [2 Corinthians 5:17]." Feelings will fluctuate, but the facts of God's Word cannot change. Here is one of those *facts*: "These things have I written unto you that believe on the name of the Son of God; that ye may know that ye have eternal life [1 John 5:13]."

There is never a need to doubt your salvation—not when you've got God's Word on it.

WINNING THE SELF-RIGHTEOUS

The self-righteous type of individual is among the most difficult to win to the Lord. He doesn't see any need to be saved. As far as he is concerned he is good enough, so why should he repent?

I once heard a man say, "I live a more honest life than some Christians I know, so why should I become a Christian?" What a sad commentary on the kind of testimony some Christians have to offer with their lives! That kind of "testimony" makes it difficult to deal with those who see themselves as "good" people—"better than some Christians"—and therefore feel no need of forgiveness and cleansing.

The self-righteous person needs to know that it is not *his* viewpoint that counts; it is God's!

God's View of the Self-Righteous

"All our righteousnesses are as filthy rags" (Isaiah 64:6). That's how God looks at an unsaved person's efforts to earn "points" with Him—no matter how good his works might be.

Christ had more than a few choice words for the self-righteous people of His day. The Pharisees really drew His fire. These were the religious leaders, the clergy, the law experts who prided themselves in their religious knowledge and activities and their sterling outward manners. They gave liberal offerings (nearly a triple tithe of their income). They read the Old Testament every day without fail and were careful to observe all the religious feasts and ceremonies. They prayed three times a day. They were moral, educated, and cultured, and they let everyone know it.

You might think the Lord would have used these fine, well-bred citizens as examples. Well, that He did. He used them as an illustration of exactly what *not* to do! Think how the Lord must have stunned His listeners when He motioned toward these heroes and said, "For I say unto you, That except your righteousness shall exceed the righteousness of the scribes and Pharisees, ye shall in no case enter into the kingdom of heaven [Matthew 5:20]."

The Lord drove His point home as "he spake this parable unto certain which trusted in themselves that they were righteous, and despised others: Two men went up into the temple to pray; the one a Pharisee, and the other a publican. The Pharisee stood and prayed thus with himself, God, I thank thee, that I am not as other men are, extortioners, unjust, adulterers, or even as this publican. I fast twice in the week, I give tithes of all that I possess. And the publican, standing afar off, would not lift up so much as his eyes unto heaven, but smote upon his breast, saying, God be merciful to me a sinner. I tell you, this man went down to his house justified rather than the other: for every one that exalteth himself shall be abased; and he that humbleth himself shall be exalted [Luke 18:9–14].

A New Birth Is Necessary

A most interesting conversation took place between Jesus and one of the most "have-it-together" men who ever lived in the city of Jerusalem. If any man could have been considered righteous, it would have been good-hearted, "super-careful-to-observe-all-the-law" Nicodemus. Who would have ever thought Jesus would have directed these words at this man: "Except a man be born again, he cannot see the kingdom of God. . . Verily, verily, I say unto thee, Except a man be born of water and of the Spirit, he cannot enter into the kingdom of God. That which is born of the flesh is flesh; and that which is born of the Spirit is spirit. Marvel not that I said unto thee, Ye must be born again [John 3:3, 5–7]."

Christ's Righteousness Alone Is Sufficient

The fact that a person must have the righteousness of *Christ* in order to be saved shows clearly that *self*-righteousness will not suffice. We are not made fit for heaven through our own goodness, but Christ's. If it be true that "all our righteousnesses are as filthy rags," then the only thing that can make us fit for the Kingdom is the righteousness of Christ. His righteousness is given freely to those who receive Him as their Savior.

Salvation Is a Free Gift

Any effort to earn salvation through good works is a supreme insult to God, who has paid a terribly high price in order to give it away. After the sacrifice of His Son, you can be very sure that no amount of good work is going to be acceptable. (How would you feel if you offered someone a gift you had paid for with the life of your only child and the person offered to pay for it?)

So, there is no such thing as a *self*-righteous person. And even if there were, *there would be no salvation available to him.* For Christ said that He did not come to call the righteous, but sinners to repentance. (See Luke 5:32.) "For the Son of man is come to seek and to save that which was lost [Luke 19:10]." Salvation is a gift given *only* to those who simply believe in the Lord Jesus Christ and humbly accept Him as their personal Savior.

When dealing with a so-called self-righteous person, point out to him that those who come into the presence of God become abruptly aware of their lack of righteousness and their sin. Three great scriptural examples of this are Job, Isaiah, and Paul (all blue ribbon, good people). Job, the successful and extremely moral businessman confessed: "I have heard of thee by the hearing of the ear; but now mine eye seeth thee: wherefore I abhor myself, and repent in dust and ashes [Job 42:5, 6]."

Isaiah the prophet had what some would consider an "inside track" with God. Yet, when this preacher's eyes beheld the Lord high and lifted up, he cried, "Woe is me! for I am undone; because I am a man of unclean lips, and I dwell in the midst of a people of unclean lips: for mine eyes have seen the King, the LORD of hosts [Isaiah 6:5]."

The apostle Paul had been a top-flight Pharisee. If any man could boast of righteousness, it would be he. But after his encounter with God on the Damascene road, he penned these lines: "Though I might also have confidence in the flesh. If any other man thinketh that he hath whereof he might trust in the flesh, I more: circumcised the eighth day, of the stock of Israel, of the tribe of Benjamin, a Hebrew of the Hebrews; as touching the righteousness which is in the law, blameless. But what things were gain to me, those I counted loss for Christ. Yea doubtless, and I count all things but loss for the excellency of the knowledge of Christ Jesus my Lord: for whom I have suffered the loss of all things, and do count them but dung, that I may win Christ, and be found in him, not having mine own righteousness, which is of the law, but that which is through the faith of Christ, the righteousness which is of God by faith [Philippians 3:4–9]."

WINNING THE PROCRASTINATOR

The "procrastinator" does not deny his need for salvation; he just rejects the idea that he needs to be saved *now*. He hopes to be saved someday before he dies. Right now, though, he wants to have fun and sow a few wild oats. He thinks there will be plenty of time later to think about eternity.

This individual needs to be shown that God places present tense priority on salvation. *Now* is the time, not later. "Come *now*, and let us reason together, saith the LORD: though your sins be as scarlet, they shall be as white as snow; though they be red like crimson, they shall be as wool [Isaiah 1:18]." "For he saith, I have heard thee in a time accepted, and in the day of salvation have I succored [helped] thee: Behold, *now* is the accepted time; behold, *now* is the day of salvation [2 Corinthians 6:2]."

Procrastination in eternal matters is a dangerous gamble. To die without Christ means eternal separation from God. Our Lord used the harshest terms to describe the awful consequence of procrastination—*perish, lost, destruction.* (See John 3:16; Luke 19:10; Matthew 7:13.)

Of course, the procrastinator just might be right; he *might* be saved sometime before he dies. One cannot argue that possibility. Procrastinators have been known to come to the Lord at the last moment for salvation. However, the procrastinator should be aware of the consequences his lack of action can bring about in his *present* life: "Whatsoever a man soweth, that shall he also reap [Galatians 6:7]," and "he that soweth to his flesh shall of the flesh reap corruption [Galatians 6:8]."

Postponing a decision to accept Christ until the last moment not only will bear negative consequences in this life, but will rule out the possibility of receiving eternal rewards at the judgment seat of Christ: "Now if any man build upon this foundation gold, silver, precious stones, wood, hay, stubble; every man's work shall be made manifest: for the day shall declare it, because it shall be revealed by fire; and the fire shall try every man's work of what sort it is. If any man's work abide which he hath built thereupon, he shall receive a reward. If any man's work shall be burned, he shall suffer loss: but he himself shall be saved; yet so as by fire [1 Corinthians 3:12–15]."

Answers to the Procrastinator's Excuses

"Not right now." "Boast not thyself of tomorrow; for thou knowest not what a day may bring forth" (Proverbs 27:1).

"Seek ye the LORD while he may be found, call ye upon him while he is near: let the wicked forsake his way, and the unrighteous man his thoughts: and let him return unto the LORD, and he will have mercy upon him; and to our God, for he will abundantly pardon [Isaiah 55:6, 7]."

"For yourselves know perfectly that the day of the Lord so cometh as a thief in the night. For when they shall say, Peace and safety; then sudden destruction cometh upon them, as travail upon a woman with child; and they shall not escape [1 Thessalonians 5:2, 3]."

"I'm too young to be concerned about religion." "Remember now thy Creator in the days of thy youth, while the evil days come not, nor the years draw nigh, when thou shalt say, I have no pleasure in them [Ecclesiastes 12:1]."

"But exhort one another daily, while it is called Today; lest any of you be hardened through the deceitfulness of sin [Hebrews 3:13]."

"Wait until I become successful in my career."   Here are two Biblical cases that show that Christ does not require self improvement as a prerequisite to salvation:

"And after these things he went forth, and saw a publican, named Levi, sitting at the receipt of custom: and he said unto him, Follow me. And he left all, rose up, and followed him. And Levi made him a great feast in his own house: and there was a great company of publicans and of others that sat down with them. But their scribes and Pharisees murmured against his disciples, saying, Why do ye eat and drink with publicans and sinners? And Jesus answering said unto them, They that are whole need not a physician; but they that are sick. I came not to call the righteous, but sinners to repentance [Luke 5:27–32]."

"And Jesus entered and passed through Jericho. And, behold, there was a man named Zaccheus, which was the chief among the publicans, and he was rich. And he sought to see Jesus who he was; and could not for the press, because he was little of stature. And he ran before, and climbed up into a sycamore tree to see him; for he was to pass that way. And when Jesus came to the place, he looked up, and saw him, and said unto him, Zaccheus, make haste, and come down; for today I must abide at thy house. And he made haste, and came down, and received him joyfully. And when they saw it, they all murmured, saying, That he was gone to be guest with a man that is a sinner. And Zaccheus stood, and said unto the Lord;

Behold, Lord, the half of my goods I give to the poor; and if I have taken any thing from any man by false accusation, I restore him fourfold. And Jesus said unto him, This day is salvation come to this house, forasmuch as he also is a son of Abraham. For the Son of man is come to seek and to save that which was lost [Luke 19:1–10]."

"The cost is too high." The person who feels he will have to give up too much of the world's pleasures and interests should be shown what the costs are of *not* coming to Christ. "For what shall it profit a man, if he shall gain the whole world, and lose his own soul? [Mark 8:36]"

R. A. Torrey used to preach a sermon entitled, "What It Costs Not To Be a Christian."* His outline should be helpful in dealing with someone who claims that turning his life over to Christ would cost him too much. According to Torrey, the costs of not being a Christian are:

1. . . . the sacrifice of peace, peace of conscience, and peace of heart.
2. . . . the sacrifice of joy, of the purest, truest, most satisfying, and most enduring joy that is found on the earth.
3. . . . the sacrifice of hope of eternal life.
4. . . . the sacrifice of the highest manhood and womanhood.
5. . . . the sacrifice of God's favor.
6. . . . the sacrifice of Christ's acknowledgement in the world to come.
7. . . . the sacrifice of eternal life, and means to perish forever.

It is clear that *not* being a Christian simply costs too much!

*R. A. Torrey, *How to Bring Men to Christ*, Minneapolis: Bethany House, 1977.

WINNING THE FEARFUL

Strange as it may seem, it is fear alone that often keeps a person from coming to Christ. The fear that "I'm not good enough; I'm too great a sinner," for example, keeps some from seeking salvation.

There may be the person who is afraid he cannot "hold out" as a Christian. This type may look wistfully at happy Christians and long to be like them. They have tried over and over again to "live right" but only seemed to fail. Or, there are those who are plagued by the fear they may have committed the unpardonable sin and that there is no hope of being saved. This paralyzing fear can keep sinners from coming to the Lord and bring sheer terror to the hearts of many Christians.

In this chapter we will look at ways people can overcome these fears that sometimes serve as gigantic roadblocks to coming to Christ.

Fear: "I Am Too Great a Sinner"

This person feels that God will not forgive his past. He has a "thousand" reasons why God just couldn't be interested in him. But his impression of God is all wrong. He thinks God's favor rests only on "good people," or those who have not committed the sins he has.

The key word to give this person is the *"whosoever"* of John 3:16. This word is all-inclusive. It means sinners—*all* sinners, including him.

Here is how you can deal with this fear:

1. Have the person read Romans 5:6–10, and ask him which of the four groups he might belong to. Point out that any of these categories are covered by the price paid for sin. "For when we were yet *without strength*, in due time Christ died for the *ungodly*. For scarcely for a righteous man will one die: yet peradventure for a good man some would even dare to die. But God commendeth his love toward us, in that, while we were yet *sinners*, Christ died for us. Much more then, being now justified by his blood, we shall be saved from wrath through him. For if, when we were *enemies*, we were reconciled to God by the death of his Son; much more, being reconciled, we shall be saved by his life."

2. Read and explain the following verses. "The Lord is not slack concerning his promise, as some men count slackness; but is long-suffering to us-ward, not willing that any should perish, but that all should come to repentance [2 Peter 3:9]." ". . . God our Savior; who will have all men to be saved, and to come unto the knowledge of the truth [1 Timothy 2:3, 4]."

3. Explain that the blood Christ shed has already been accepted as full payment by God the Father for his sin. "Forasmuch as ye know that ye were not redeemed with the corruptible things, as silver and gold, from your vain conversation received by tradition from your fathers; but with the precious blood of Christ, as of a lamb without blemish and without spot [1 Peter 1:18, 19]."

   Have you ever received this kind of announcement in the mail? *"You, Mr. Prospect, may have already won the grand prize. The number has already been selected, and if that number is yours, all you have to do is claim your prize."* Well, salvation is the grand prize. And there's no question or doubt involved. You, "Mr. Prospect," HAVE won eternal life. All you have to do is *claim* your gift through Christ Jesus who has already paid for it.

4. Remind the person that God has already saved some pretty "bad" sinners. David is a good example. He had committed

adultery and then murdered the husband to cover his crime. (The Watergate cover-up was nothing compared with that one!)

No one is beyond the reach of Christ's saving grace. Jesus is willing to say to anyone, just as He said to the sinful woman who washed His feet with her tears, "[Thy] sins are forgiven. . . thy faith hath saved thee; go in peace." (See Luke 7:37–50.)

The Corinthian church was not exactly a day care center for cheribs. It consisted of a congregation of sin-scarred people who were saved out of a morass of immorality and heathenistic worship. The apostle Paul once reminded these people that before they came to Christ, the grievous sins some of them had committed would have kept them out of heaven. But now, according to Paul, they had been washed, sanctified, and justified "in the name of the Lord Jesus, and by the Spirit of our God [1 Corinthians 6:11]."

5. Point out that even though he may have rejected God over and over again, he can still come. God still wants him. Assure him that even the slightest desire he may have to now come to God is there because the Holy Spirit put it there. Remind him of Christ's words, "[He] that cometh to me I will in no wise cast out [John 6:37]."

Fear: "I Cannot Hold Out"

Who says *you* have to? The power to hold out has its source in *Christ*, not us. "But as many as received him, to them gave he power to become the sons of God, even to them that believe on his name [John 1:12]."

This source of power is not temporary, but continuous: "Wherefore he is able also to save them to the uttermost that come unto God by him, seeing he ever liveth to make intercession for them [Hebrews 7:25]."

Paul describes a very interesting personal predicament in Romans 7:15–8:2. He very candidly relates his own struggle (and victory) over the problem of holding out: "I don't understand myself at all, for I really want to do what is right, but I can't. I do what I don't want to—what I hate. I know perfectly well that what I am doing is wrong, and my bad conscience proves that I agree with these laws I am breaking. But I can't help myself, because I'm no longer doing it. It is sin inside me that is stronger than I am that makes me do these evil things. I know I am rotten through and through so far as my old sinful nature is concerned. No matter which way I turn I can't make myself do right. I want to but I can't. When I want to do good, I don't; and when I try not to do wrong, I do it anyway. Now if I am doing what I don't want to, it is plain where the trouble is: sin still has me in its evil grasp. It seems to be a fact of life that when I want to do what is right, I inevitably do what is wrong. I love to do God's will so far as my new nature is concerned; but there is something else deep within me, in my lower nature, that is at war with my mind and wins the fight and makes me a slave to the sin that is still within me. In my mind I want to be God's willing servant but instead I find myself still enslaved to sin. So you see how it is: my new life tells me to do right, but the old nature that is still inside me loves to sin. Oh, what a terrible predicament I'm in! Who will free me from my slavery to this deadly lower nature? Thank God! It has been done by Jesus Christ our Lord. He has set me free. So there is now no condemnation awaiting those who belong to Christ Jesus. For the power of the life-giving Spirit—and this power is mine through Christ Jesus—has freed me from the vicious circle of sin and death [*Living Bible*]."

Paul then revealed the bottom line secret to "holding out" in Romans 8:6–9: "Following after the Holy Spirit leads to life and peace, but following after the old nature leads to death, because the old sinful nature within us is against God. It never did obey God's laws and it never will. That's why those who are still under the control of their old sinful selves, bent on following their old evil desires, can never please God. But you are not like that. You are controlled by your new nature if you have the Spirit of God living in you. (And remember that if anyone doesn't have the Spirit of Christ living in him, he is not a Christian at all.) [*Living Bible*]."

Fear: "I Have Committed the Unpardonable Sin"

Probably no other fear is more paralyzing than the belief that one has committed the unpardonable sin. It would be difficult for most of us to comprehend the emotional trauma, the desperation that comes over those who feel they can never be forgiven; that they are doomed to be lost no matter what they do. Some individuals have been known to develop a definite psychosis because of thinking they had committed this dreadful sin.

There are two things to avoid when counseling a person who fears he or she has committed the unpardonable sin: (1) Never take for granted that this damnable sin has actually been committed, and (2) never tell anyone he or she has committed this sin. You may be wrong, and making such a statement would only plunge them deeper into despair.

Reverend G. Raymond Carlson, the assistant general

superintendent of the Assemblies of God, has written an excellent examination of the subject of the unpardonable sin, and I wish to devote the remainder of this chapter to his article that appeared in the May 8, 1983 issue of the *Pentecostal Evangel.* Mr. Carlson wrote:

> We find six Scripture verses that deal with sinning against the Holy Spirit.
>
> One, *blasphemy* against the Holy Spirit, is identified in the Gospels (Matthew 12:24–32; Mark 3:22–30).
>
> Two are mentioned in the Acts—*lying* to the Spirit (5:3, 4) and *resisting* the Spirit (7:51).
>
> Three are found in the Epistles—*grieving* (Ephesians 4:30), *quenching* (1 Thessalonians 5:19), and *insulting* or doing despite to the Spirit (Hebrews 10:29).
>
> Three of the above admonitions relate to the unbeliever—*blaspheming, resisting,* and *insulting.* The other three—*lying to, grieving,* and *quenching*—relate to the believer.
>
> All are serious offenses. Ananias and Sapphira paid an awful price for *lying* to the Spirit (Acts 5:1–10). To be guilty of *grieving* or *quenching* the Spirit can readily rob the believer of his joy and victory.
>
> Before we are converted, the Holy Spirit deals with us to convict us of sin and draw us to Christ. If we turn away from His wooings, we *resist* Him, which is to risk eternal loss. Some go beyond this to *insult* Him which will bring "sorer punishment" than those who "despised Moses' law and died without mercy [Hebrews 10:28, 29]."
>
> Others go to the extreme and *blaspheme the Spirit.* To blaspheme is to commit spiritual suicide. This is the

unpardonable sin. When this sin is committed, there is no repentance or forgiveness. The results are so drastic that it is of upmost importance that we define this sin correctly.

Jesus declared, "All manner of sin and blasphemy shall be forgiven unto men: but the blasphemy against the Holy Ghost shall not be forgiven unto men. And whosoever speaketh a word against the Son of man, it shall be forgiven him: but whosoever speaketh against the Holy Ghost, it shall not be forgiven him, neither in this world, neither in the world to come [Matthew 12:31, 32]."

The New International Version translates Mark 3:28–30: " 'I tell you the truth, all the sins and blasphemies of men will be forgiven them. But whoever blasphemes against the Holy Spirit will never be forgiven; he is guilty of an eternal sin.' He said this because they were saying, 'He has an evil spirit.' "

What an appalling thought! There is a sin which can never be forgiven in this life or the one to come! What then is this sin? To find out, let us first ascertain what it is not.

The unpardonable sin is not sin that is done in ignorance. The apostle Paul wrote that before his conversion he was "a blasphemer . . . but I obtained mercy, because I did it ignorantly in unbelief [1 Timothy 1:13]."

Neither is it the sin of resisting the Holy Spirit. That sin is pardonable. The martyr Stephen said, "Ye stiffnecked and uncircumcised in heart and ears, ye do always resist the Holy Ghost: as your fathers did, so do ye" (Acts 7:51). At least one of those so denounced by Stephen as being guilty of resisting the Spirit found repentance; for Saul of Tarsus was in that company and later he was saved and filled with the Spirit.

The unpardonable sin is more than sinning away the day of grace by procrastination. To reject the Lord Jesus Christ is not an act of sin for which there is no forgiveness. Many have rejected, as did Saul of Tarsus, but later have repented and found salvation.

The sin of unbelief, which may persist until death, is not in the category of the "eternal sin" which is irrevocably beyond repentance. The sin of unbelief does bring the wrath of God upon the unbeliever. As long as we continue in unbelief, we remain unsaved and under condemnation (John 3:36). But unbelief is not an act of sin for which there is no forgiveness. It is pardoned when the unbeliever becomes a believer.

Some people become extremely concerned, fearing that they have committed the unpardonable sin. People have come to me in utter panic—weeping uncontrollably—thinking there was no forgiveness for them. Some have been so harassed by the thought that they have attempted suicide or have needed to be confined to a hospital for the insane. Such persons have not committed the "eternal sin." If they had, they would not be so greatly concerned about it.

All blasphemy against the Holy Spirit is sin; but all sin against the Spirit is not blasphemy. Provision has been made for every sin, no matter how vile, at Calvary. There is even provision for blasphemy against Christ (Matthew 12:32); and all offenses against the Holy Spirit can be forgiven, except blasphemy.

Blasphemy is the "expression of contempt for the personality and authority of deity, and grossly unworthy conduct in the face of the divine," according to L. Thomas Holdcroft.

The sin of blasphemy against the Spirit is unpardonable but not because of some arbitrary decree of God, for He is eternally a God of infinite mercy and grace (2 Peter 3:9; Matthew 11:28). In other words, the unavailability of forgiveness is not due to any lack in Christ's provision at Calvary, nor a lack in God's ability to extend grace, nor His unwillingness to pardon. It rests rather in the fact that the sin itself makes pardon impossible.

Our salvation is the result of the work of the Trinity. The Father planned it, the Son provided it, and the Holy Spirit brings it about. The work of the Father and the Son is completed. The Holy Spirit, as the divine Administrator, has a continuing work until the saved are gathered home at Christ's coming to receive His church.

The Holy Spirit conveys the benefits of Calvary to us. He presents the good tidings of salvation, convicts us of sin, and enables us to repent and to exercise faith. The Spirit is the lifeline between God and us. We cut off the lifeline if we blaspheme against the Spirit.

Our only way through Christ to the Father is by the Spirit. He convicts us, draws us, woos us, and makes our hearts responsive to the preaching of the gospel. No man can even say with a true confession that Jesus is Lord except by the Holy Spirit (1 Corinthians 12:3).

Since the Spirit is the One who implants the life of Christ in us, rejection of the Spirit is rejection of that life. To reject and despise the Spirit is to reject God's only means of showing His grace to us.

What Jesus spoke of was not one isolated act but a deliberate course of continuing action which culminates in a condition which places a person irrevocably outside of God's ability to forgive.

It is an act of spiritual suicide. The sin is unpardonable not because God is angry nor because He refuses to forgive. The act is such that it puts God in a position where He cannot forgive.

This spiritual suicide is the result of malicious perversion and persistent opposition to the known truth about God's acts of mercy and grace. It is a choice made with conscious deliberation and without compunction, remorse, or shame. The person who follows this course is utterly impenitent.

To ascribe the works of the Holy Spirit to the devil and demon power cuts the lifeline, for only the Spirit can bridge the gulf of unbelief. To be guilty of the ultimate sin of blasphemy is to be guilty of "an eternal sin."

Let it be said again that as long as a person has the desire and the determination to obtain salvation, it is possible for him to do so. For the Bible declares, "Whosoever shall call upon the name of the Lord shall be saved [Romans 10:13]."

SCRIPTURE "FIRST AID KIT"

Although winning a family member—or anyone—to Christ is a process (rather than a simple matter of technique), there have been instances when a person was won as a direct and immediate result of a family member or friend applying the right scriptural treatment to the wound of personal need. There will be times when the one you wish to win to Christ will suffer a loss, face an important decision, or contemplate a serious question. During this time he may ask, as David did, "From whence cometh my help?" You need to be ready to show him that his "help cometh from the Lord."

Sometimes just a little first aid treatment from the Word can do overnight what days of "witnessing" seem unable to do. This section is offered as a Scripture "first aid kit" for the hurts, sorrows, and questions of your family members and friends. Please apply with prayer.

First Aid for Anxiety

Psalm 55:22.   "Cast thy burden upon the Lord, and he shall sustain thee: he shall never suffer the righteous to be moved."

Matthew 6:33, 34.   "But seek ye first the kingdom of God, and his righteousness; and all these things shall be added unto you. Take therefore no thought for the morrow: for the morrow shall take thought for the things of itself. Sufficient unto the day is the evil thereof."

Philippians 4:6, 7.   "Don't worry about anything; instead, pray about everything; tell God your needs and don't forget to thank him for his answers. If you do this you will experience God's peace, which is far more wonderful than the human mind can understand. His peace will keep your thoughts and your hearts quiet and at rest as you trust in Christ Jesus" [*Living Bible*].

1 Peter 5:7.   "Casting all your care upon him; for he careth for you."

First Aid for Bereavement

Psalm 23:4, 6.   "Yea, though I walk through the valley of the shadow of death, I will fear no evil: for thou art with me; thy rod and thy staff they comfort me . . . Surely goodness and mercy shall follow me all the days of my life: and I will dwell in the house of the Lord for ever."

John 11:25.   "Jesus said unto her, I am the resurrection, and the life: he that believeth in me, though he were dead, yet shall he live."

John 14:1–3.   "Let not your heart be troubled: ye believe in God, believe also in me. In my Father's house are many mansions: if it were not so, I would have told you. I go to prepare a place for you. And if I go and prepare a place for you, I will come again, and receive you unto myself; that where I am, there ye may be also."

1 Corinthians 13:12.   "For now we see through a glass, darkly, but then face to face: now I know in part; but then shall I know even as also I am known."

2 Corinthians 5:1.   "For we know that, if our earthly house of this tabernacle were dissolved, we have a building of God, a house not made with hands, eternal in the heavens."

Philippians 1:21.   "For me to live is Christ, and to die is gain."

1 Peter 1:3, 4.   "Blessed be the God and Father of our Lord Jesus Christ, which according to his abundant mercy hath begotten us again unto a lively hope by the resurrection of Jesus Christ from the dead, to an inheritance incorruptible, and undefiled, and that fadeth not away, reserved in heaven for you."

First Aid for Bereavement: Dealing with Grief

Isaiah 43:2.   "When thou passest through the waters, I will be with thee; and through the rivers, they shall not overflow thee: when thou walkest through the fire, thou shalt not be burned; neither shall the flame kindle upon thee."

Matthew 5:4. "Blessed are they that mourn: for they shall be comforted."

2 Corinthians 1:3–5. "Blessed be God, even the Father of our Lord Jesus Christ, the Father of mercies, and the God of all comfort; who comforteth us in all our tribulation, that we may be able to comfort them which are in any trouble, by the comfort wherewith we ourselves are comforted of God. For as the sufferings of Christ abound in us, so our consolation also aboundeth by Christ."

2 Corinthians 1:9. "But we had the sentence of death in ourselves, that we should not trust in ourselves, but in God which raiseth the dead."

2 Timothy 1:12. "For the which cause I also suffer these things: nevertheless I am not ashamed; for I know whom I have believed, and am persuaded that he is able to keep that which I have committed unto him against that day."

First Aid for Bereavement:
Losing One's Mate

Job 12:10. "In whose hand is the soul of every living thing, and the breath of all mankind."

Job 13:15. "Though he slay me, yet will I trust in him."

Job 14:5. "Seeing his days are determined, the number of his months are with thee, thou hast appointed his bounds that he cannot pass."

Job 23:10. "But he knoweth the way that I take: when he hath tried me, I shall come forth as gold."

Psalm 145:18. "The Lord is nigh unto all them that call upon him, to all that call upon him in truth."

Psalm 146:9. "The Lord preserveth the strangers; he relieveth the fatherless and widow: but the way of the wicked he turneth upside down."

Jeremiah 29:11. "For I know the plans I have for you, says the Lord. They are plans for good and not for evil, to give you a future and a hope" [*Living Bible*].

Revelation 21:4. "And God shall wipe away all tears from their eyes; and there shall be no more death, neither sorrow, nor crying, neither shall there be any more pain: for the former things are passed away."

First Aid for Bitterness

Matthew 6:14, 15. "For if ye forgive men their trespasses, your heavenly Father will also forgive you: but if ye forgive not men their trespasses, neither will your Father forgive your trespasses."

Luke 23:34. "Then said Jesus, Father, forgive them; for they know not what they do. And they parted his raiment, and cast lots."

Romans 12:14, 17–19. "Bless them which persecute you: bless, and curse not . . . Recompense to no man evil for evil. Provide things honest in the sight of all men. If it be possible, as much as lieth in you, live peaceably with all men. Dearly beloved, avenge not yourselves, but rather give place unto wrath: for it is written, Vengeance is mine; I will repay, saith the Lord."

Ephesians 4:31, 32. "Let all bitterness, and wrath, and anger, and clamor, and evil speaking, be put away from you, with all malice: and be ye kind one to another, tender-hearted, forgiving one another, even as God for Christ's sake hath forgiven you."

Hebrews 12:14, 15. "Follow peace with all men, and holiness, without which no man shall see the Lord: looking diligently lest any man fail of the grace of God; lest any root of bitterness springing up trouble you, and thereby many be defiled."

1 Peter 2:23. "Who, when he was reviled, reviled not again; when he suffered, he threatened not; but committed himself to him that judgeth righteously."

First Aid for Undergoing Chastening

Job 5:17. "Behold, happy is the man whom God correcteth: therefore despise not thou the chastening of the Almighty."

Psalm 94:12, 13. "Blessed is the man whom thou chasteneth, O Lord, and teachest him out of thy law; that thou mayest give him rest from the days of adversity, until the pit be digged for the wicked."

Psalm 119:67, 71. "Before I was afflicted I went astray: but now have I kept thy word. . . . It is good for me that I have been afflicted; that I might learn thy statutes."

Proverbs 3:11, 12. "My son, despise not the chastening of the Lord; neither be weary of his correction: for whom the Lord loveth he correcteth; even as a father the son in whom he delighteth."

2 Corinthians 12:7. "And lest I should be exalted above measure through the abundance of the revelations, there was given to me a thorn in the flesh, the messenger of Satan to buffet me, lest I should be exalted above measure."

Hebrews 12:5–11. "And ye have forgotten the exhortation which speaketh unto you as unto children, My son, despise not thou the chastening of the Lord, nor faint when thou art rebuked of him. . . . If ye endure chastening, God dealeth with you as with sons; for what son is he whom the father chasteneth not? But if ye be without chastisement, whereof all are partakers, then are ye bastards, and not sons. Furthermore, we have had fathers of our flesh which corrected us, and we gave them reverence: shall we not much rather be in subjection unto the Father of spirits, and live? For they verily for a few days chastened us after their own pleasure; but he for our profit, that we might be partakers of his holiness. Now no chastening for the present seemeth to be joyous, but grievous: nevertheless, afterward it yieldeth the peaceable fruit of righteousness unto them which are exercised thereby."

Revelation 3:19. "As many as I love, I rebuke and chasten: be zealous therefore, and repent."

First Aid for Fear of Death

Psalm 23:4. "Yea, though I walk through the valley of the shadow of death, I will fear no evil: for thou art with me; thy rod and thy staff they comfort me."

John 11:25. "Jesus said unto her, I am the resurrection, and the life: he that believeth in me, though he were dead, yet shall he live."

John 14:1–3. "Let not your heart be troubled: ye believe in God, believe also in me. In my Father's house are many mansions: if it were not so, I would have told you. I go to prepare a place for you. And if I go and prepare a place for you, I will come again, and receive you unto myself; that where I am, there ye may be also."

1 Corinthians 2:9, 10. "But as it is written, Eye hath not seen, nor ear heard, neither have entered into the heart of man, the things which God hath prepared for them that love him. But God hath revealed them unto us by his Spirit: for the Spirit searcheth all things, yea, the deep things of God."

1 Corinthians 15:54. "So when this corruptible shall have put on incorruption, and this mortal shall have put on immortality, then shall be brought to pass the saying that is written, Death is swallowed up in victory."

2 Corinthians 5:1. "For we know that, if our earthly house of this tabernacle were dissolved, we have a building of God, a house not made with hands, eternal in the heavens."

Philippians 1:21. "For to me to live is Christ, and to die is gain."

Philippians 3:20, 21. "For our conversation is in heaven; from whence also we look for the Savior, the Lord Jesus Christ: who shall change our vile body, that it may be fashioned like unto his glorious body, according to the working whereby he is able even to subdue all things unto himself."

2 Timothy 1:10. "Our Savior Jesus Christ, who hath abolished death, and hath brought life and immortality to light through the gospel."

First Aid for Depression or Discouragement

Psalm 27:13, 14.   "I had fainted, unless I had believed to see the goodness of the Lord in the land of the living. Wait on the Lord: be of good courage, and he shall strengthen thine heart: wait, I say, on the Lord."

Psalm 51:3, 12.   "For I acknowledge my transgressions: and my sin is ever before me. . . . Restore unto me the joy of thy salvation; and uphold me with thy free Spirit."

Isaiah 41:10.   "Fear thou not; for I am with thee: be not dismayed; for I am thy God: I will strengthen thee; yea, I will help thee; yea, I will uphold thee with the right hand of my righteousness."

Matthew 11:28–30.   "Come unto me, all ye that labor and are heavy laden, and I will give you rest. Take my yoke upon you, and learn of me; for I am meek and lowly in heart: and ye shall find rest unto your souls. For my yoke is easy, and my burden is light."

Mark 11:25.   "And when ye stand praying, forgive, if ye have aught against any; that your Father also which is in heaven may forgive you your trespasses."

Philippians 4:13.   "I can do all things through Christ which strengtheneth me."

1 Thessalonians 5:18.   "In every thing give thanks: for this is the will of God in Christ Jesus concerning you."

2 Timothy 1:7. "For God hath not given us the spirit of fear; but of power, and of love, and of a sound mind."

First Aid for Fear

Psalm 27:1, 5. "The Lord is my light and my salvation; whom shall I fear? The Lord is the strength of my life; of whom shall I be afraid? . . . For in the time of trouble he shall hide me in his pavilion: in the secret of his tabernacle shall he hide me; he shall set me upon a rock."

Psalm 34:4. "I sought the Lord, and he heard me, and delivered me from all my fears."

Proverbs 1:33. "But whoso hearkeneth unto me shall dwell safely, and shall be quiet from fear of evil."

Isaiah 35:4. "Say to them that are of a fearful heart, Be strong, fear not: behold, your God will come with vengeance, even God with a recompense; he will come and save you."

Isaiah 41:10. "Fear thou not; for I am with thee: be not dismayed; for I am thy God: I will strengthen thee; yea, I will help thee; yea, I will uphold thee with the right hand of my righteousness."

Isaiah 43:2. "When thou passest through the waters, I will be with thee; and through the rivers, they shall not overflow thee: when thou walkest through the fire, thou shalt not be burned; neither shall the flame kindle upon thee."

Romans 8:15. "For ye have not received the spirit of bondage again to fear; but ye have received the Spirit of adoption, whereby we cry, Abba, Father."

2 Timothy 1:7. "For God hath not given us the spirit of fear; but of power, and of love, and of a sound mind."

Hebrews 13:5, 6. "He hath said, I will never leave thee, nor forsake thee. So that we may boldly say, The Lord is my helper, and I will not fear what man shall do unto me."

1 John 4:18. "There is no fear in love; but perfect love casteth out fear: because fear hath torment. He that feareth is not made perfect in love."

First Aid for Financial Difficulty

Psalm 37:25. "I [David] have been young, and now am old; yet have I not seen the righteous forsaken, nor his seed begging bread."

Malachi 3:8–10. "Will a man rob God? Yet ye have robbed me. But ye say, Wherein have we robbed thee? In tithes and offerings. Ye are cursed with a curse: for ye have robbed me, even this whole nation. Bring ye all the tithes into the storehouse, that there may be meat in mine house, and prove me now herewith, saith the Lord of hosts, if I will not open you the windows of heaven, and pour you out a blessing, that there shall not be room enough to receive it."

Matthew 6:33. "But seek ye first the kingdom of God, and his righteousness; and all these things shall be added unto you."

Philippians 4:19. "But my God shall supply all your need according to his riches in glory by Christ Jesus."

1 John 5:14, 15. "And this is the confidence that we have in him, that, if we ask any thing according to his will, he heareth us: and if we know that he hear us, whatsoever we ask, we know that we have the petitions that we desired of him."

First Aid for Guilt

Isaiah 44:22. "I have blotted out, as a thick cloud, thy transgressions, and, as a cloud, thy sins: return unto me; for I have redeemed thee."

John 8:36. "If the Son therefore shall make you free, ye shall be free indeed."

Romans 8:1. "There is therefore now no condemnation to them which are in Christ Jesus, who walk not after the flesh, but after the Spirit."

Philippians 3:13, 14. "But this one thing I do, forgetting those things which are behind, and reaching forth unto those things which are before, I press toward the mark for the prize of the high calling of God in Christ Jesus."

Hebrews 8:12. "For I will be merciful to their unrighteousness, and their sins and their iniquities will I remember no more."

First Aid for Hopelessness

Psalm 27:13, 14. "I had fainted, unless I had believed to see the goodness of the Lord in the land of the living. Wait on the Lord: be of good courage, and he shall strengthen thine heart: wait, I say, on the Lord."

Psalm 42:11. "Why art thou cast down, O my soul? And why art thou disquieted within me? Hope thou in God: for I shall yet praise him, who is the health of my countenance, and my God."

Jeremiah 17:7. "Blessed is the man that trusteth in the Lord, and whose hope the Lord is."

Romans 15:13. "Now the God of hope fill you with all joy and peace in believing, that ye may abound in hope, through the power of the Holy Ghost."

2 Corinthians 4:8–10. "We are troubled on every side, yet not distressed; we are perplexed, but not in despair; persecuted, but not forsaken; cast down, but not destroyed; always bearing about in the body the dying of the Lord Jesus, that the life also of Jesus might be made manifest in our body."

First Aid for Impatience

Job 23:10. "But he knoweth the way that I take: when he hath tried me, I shall come forth as gold."

Psalm 37:7. "Rest in the Lord, and wait patiently for him: fret not thyself because of him who prospereth in his way, because of the man who bringeth wicked devices to pass."

Psalm 40:1. "I waited patiently for the Lord; and he inclined unto me, and heard my cry."

Isaiah 40:31. "But they that wait upon the Lord shall renew their strength; they shall mount up with wings as eagles; they shall run, and not be weary; and they shall walk, and not faint."

Romans 5:3–5. "We glory in tribulations also; knowing that tribulation worketh patience; and patience, experience; and experience, hope: and hope maketh not ashamed; because the love of God is shed abroad in our hearts by the Holy Ghost which is given unto us."

Romans 8:25. "But if we hope for that we see not, then do we with patience wait for it."

Romans 12:12. "Rejoicing in hope; patient in tribulation; continuing instant in prayer."

Philippians 4:11. "Not that I speak in respect of want: for

I have learned, in whatsoever state I am, therewith to be content."

Hebrews 10:35, 36. "Cast not away therefore your confidence, which hath great recompense of reward. For ye have need of patience, that, after ye have done the will of God, ye might receive the promise."

James 1:2–4. "My brethren, count it all joy when ye fall into divers temptations; knowing this, that the trying of your faith worketh patience. But let patience have her perfect work, that ye may be perfect and entire, wanting nothing."

James 5:7, 8. "Be patient therefore, brethren, unto the coming of the Lord. Behold, the husbandman waiteth for the precious fruit of the earth, and hath long patience for it, until he receive the early and latter rain. Be ye also patient; stablish your hearts: for the coming the Lord draweth nigh."

First Aid for Sickness

Psalm 66:18. "If I regard iniquity in my heart, the Lord will not hear me."

Matthew 18:19. "Again I say unto you, That if two of you shall agree on earth as touching any thing that they shall ask, it shall be done for them of my Father which is in heaven."

2 Corinthians 12:7–9. "And lest I [Paul] should be exalted above measure through the abundance of the revelations, there was given to me a thorn in the flesh, the messenger of Satan to buffet me, lest I should be exalted above measure. For this thing I besought the Lord thrice, that it might depart from me. And he said unto me, My grace is sufficient for thee: for my strength is made perfect in weakness. Most gladly therefore will I rather glory in my infirmities, that the power of Christ may rest upon me."

James 1:6. "But let him ask in faith, nothing wavering: for he that wavereth is like a wave of the sea driven with the wind and tossed."

James 5:13–16. "Is any among you afflicted? let him pray. Is any merry? let him sing psalms. Is any sick among you? let him call for the elders of the church; and let them pray over him, anointing him with oil in the name of the Lord: and the prayer of faith shall save the sick, and the Lord shall raise him up; and if he have committed sins, they shall be forgiven him. Confess your faults one to another, and pray for one another, that ye may be healed. The effectual fervent prayer of a righteous man availeth much."

First Aid for Suffering

Isaiah 43:2. "When thou passest through the waters, I will be with thee; and through the rivers, they shall not overflow thee: when thou walkest through the fire, thou shalt not be burned; neither shall the flame kindle upon thee."

John 16:33. "These things I have spoken unto you, that in me ye might have peace. In the world ye shall have tribulation: but be of good cheer; I have overcome the world."

Romans 8:28. "And we know that all things work together for good to them that love God, to them who are the called according to his purpose."

Romans 8:35–39. "Who shall separate us from the love of Christ? shall tribulation, or distress, or persecution, or famine, or nakedness, or peril, or sword? . . . Nay, in all these things we are more than conquerors through him that loved us. For I am persuaded, that neither death, nor life, nor angels, nor principalities, nor powers, nor things present, nor things to come, nor height, nor depth, nor any other creature, shall be able to separate us from the love of God, which is in Christ Jesus our Lord."

1 Peter 4:12, 13. "Beloved, think it not strange concerning the fiery trial which is to try you, as though some strange thing happened unto you: but rejoice, inasmuch as ye are partakers of Christ's sufferings; that, when his glory shall be revealed, ye may be glad also with exceeding joy."

Revelation 21:4. "And God shall wipe away all tears from their eyes; and there shall be no more death, neither sorrow, nor crying, neither shall there be any more pain: for the former things are passed away."

First Aid for Temptation

Matthew 4:1–4, 11. "Then was Jesus led up of the Spirit into the wilderness to be tempted of the devil. And when he had fasted forty days and forty nights, he was afterward ahungered. And when the tempter came to him, he said, If thou be the Son of God, command that these stones be made bread. But he answered and said, It is written, Man shall not live by bread alone, but by every word that proceedeth out of the mouth of God. . . .Then the devil leaveth him, and, behold, angels came and ministered unto him."

1 Corinthians 10:13. "There hath no temptation taken you but such as is common to man: but God is faithful, who will not suffer you to be tempted above that ye are able; but will with the temptation also make a way to escape, that ye may be able to bear it."

James 1:12–15. "Blessed is the man that endureth temptation: for when he is tried, he shall receive the crown of life, which the Lord hath promised to them that love him. Let no man say when he is tempted, I am tempted of God: for God cannot be tempted with evil, neither tempteth he any man: but every man is tempted, when he is drawn away of his own lust, and enticed. Then when lust hath conceived, it bringeth forth sin; and sin, when it is finished, bringeth forth death."

First Aid for Turmoil

Psalm 4:8. "I will both lay me down in peace, and sleep: for thou, Lord, only makest me dwell in safety."

Psalm 34:14. "Depart from evil, and do good; seek peace, and pursue it."

Psalm 119:165. "Great peace have they which love thy law: and nothing shall offend them."

Isaiah 26:3. "Thou wilt keep him in perfect peace, whose mind is stayed on thee: because he trusteth in thee."

Isaiah 48:18. "O that thou hadst hearkened to my commandments! then had thy peace been as a river, and thy righteousness as the waves of the sea."

John 14:27. "Peace I leave with you, my peace I give unto you: not as the world giveth, give I unto you. Let not your heart be troubled, neither let it be afraid."

John 16:33. "These things I have spoken unto you, that in me ye might have peace. In the world ye shall have tribulation: but be of good cheer; I have overcome the world."

Romans 8:6. "For to be carnally minded is death; but to be spiritually minded is life and peace."

Romans 14:17, 19. "For the kingdom of God is not meat and drink; but righteousness, and peace, and joy in the Holy Ghost. . . . Let us therefore follow after the things which make for peace, and things wherewith one may edify another."

Philippians 4:6, 7. "Be careful for nothing; but in every thing by prayer and supplication with thanksgiving let your requests be made known unto God. And the peace of God, which passeth all understanding, shall keep your hearts and minds through Christ Jesus."

Colossians 3:15. "And let the peace of God rule in your hearts, to the which also ye are called in one body; and be ye thankful."

Hebrews 12:14. "Follow peace with all men, and holiness, without which no man shall see the Lord."

First Aid for Weakness

Deuteronomy 33:25. "Thy shoes shall be iron and brass; and as thy days, so shall thy strength be."

Psalm 31:24. "Be of good courage, and he shall strengthen your heart, all ye that hope in the Lord."

Isaiah 40:28–31. "Hast thou not known? hast thou not heard, that the everlasting God, the Lord, the Creator of the ends of the earth, fainteth not, neither is weary? there is no searching of his understanding. He giveth power to the faint; and to them that have no might he increaseth strength. Even the youths shall faint and be weary, and the young men shall utterly fall: but they that wait upon the Lord shall renew their strength; they shall mount up with wings as eagles; they shall run, and not be weary; and they shall walk, and not faint."

Isaiah 41:10. "Fear thou not; for I am with thee: be not dismayed; for I am thy God: I will strengthen thee; yea, I will help thee; yea, I will uphold thee with the right hand of my righteousness."

2 Corinthians 12:9, 10. "And he said unto me, My grace is sufficient for thee: for my strength is made perfect in weakness. Most gladly therefore will I rather glory in my infirmities, that the power of Christ may rest upon me. Therefore I take pleasure in infirmities, in reproaches, in necessities, in persecutions, in distresses for Christ's sake: for when I am weak, then am I strong."

Ephesians 3:16. "That he would grant you, according to the riches of his glory, to be strengthened with might by his Spirit in the inner man."

Philippians 4:13. "I can do all things through Christ which strengtheneth me."

BIBLIOGRAPHY

Aldridge, Joseph C. *Lifestyle Evangelism.* Portland, Oregon: Multnomah, 1981.

Begbie, Harold *Twice-Born Men.* Westwood, N.J.: Revell, 1909.

Berry, Jo. *Beloved Unbeliever.* Grand Rapids: Zondervan, 1981.

Cartwright, Lin. *Evangelism for Today.* St. Louis: The Bethany Press, 1984.

Chafer, L. S. *True Evangelism.* New York: Gospel Publishing House, 1911.

Chapman, J. Wilbur. *The Personal Touch.* Westwood, N.J.: Revell, 2nd edition.

Conant, J. E *Every Member Evangelism.* New York: Harper Brothers Publishers, 1922.

Dewitt, David. *Answering the Tough Ones.* Chicago: Moody Press, 1980.

Evans, William. *Personal Soul-Winning.* Chicago: Moody Press, 1948.

Fletcher, Lionel B. *The Effective Evangelist.* London: Hodder & Stroughton, 1923.

Ford, Leighton. *The Christian Persuader.* New York: Harper & Row, 1966.

Forder, Reg. *Soulwinning.* Englewood Cliffs, N.J.: Prentice-Hall, Inc., 1984.

Goodell, Charles L. *Motives and Methods of Modern Evangelism.* Westwood, N.J.: Revell, 1907.

Graham, Billy. *Peace with God.* Westwood, N.J.: Revell, 1968.

Handford, Elizabeth Rice. *Woman in Despair.* Englewood Cliffs, N.J.: Prentice-Hall, 1982.

Harrison, Eugene Myers & Walter L. Wilson. *How to Win Souls.* Chicago: Scripture Press, 1952.

Hicks, Jos. P. *Ten Lessons in Personal Evangelism.* New York: George H. Doran Co., 1922.

Jowett, J. H. *The Passion for Souls.* New York: Revell, 1905.

Kennedy, Dennis James. *Evangelism Explosion.* Wheaton, Ill.: Tyndale House Publishers, 1970.

Krupp, Nate. *A World to Win.* Minneapolis: Bethany Fellowship, 1966.

————. *Bible Studies for Soul Winners.* Harrison, Arkansas: New Leaf Publishers, 1979.

————. *You Can Be a Soul-Winner—Here's How.* Marion, Indiana: Ly Evangelism, Inc., 1962.

Leete, F. D. *Every-Day Evangelism.* Cincinnati: Jennings and Graham, 1909.

Little, Paul E. *How to Give Away Your Faith.* Chicago: Inter-Varsity Press, 1966.

Mabie, H. C. *Methods in Soul-Winning.* Westwood, N.J.: Revell, 1906.

Manning, Doug. *With God at Your Side.* Englewood Cliffs, N.J.: Prentice-Hall, Inc., 1984.

Martin, Walter Ralston. *The Kingdom of the Cults.* Grand Rapids: Zondervan Publishing House, 1977.

Middlebrook, J. D. and Larry Summers. *The Church and Family.* Springfield, Mo.: Gospel Publishing House, 1980.

Oliver, G. F. *Soul-Winners' Secrets.* New York: Jennings and Pye, 1902.

Petersen, Jim. *Evangelism As a Lifestyle.* Colorado Springs: Navpress, 1980.

Pippert, Rebecca Manley. *Out of the Salt Shaker and Into the World.* Downers Grove, Illinois: Inter-Varsity Press, 1979.

Prince, Matthew. *Winning Through Caring.* Grand Rapids: Baker Book House, 1981.

Riggs, Ralph M. et al., *So Send I You.* Springfield, Mo.: Gospel Publishing House, 1965.

Rusthoi, Ralph W. *Soul Winning Course.* Montrose, California, 1960.

Scarborough, L. R. *How Jesus Won Men.* New York: George H. Doran Co., 1926.

Spurgeon, C. H. *The Soul-Winner.* Grand Rapids: Zondervan, 1948.

Steele, James W. *Bible Solutions to Problems of Daily Living.* Englewood Cliffs, N.J.: Prentice-Hall, Inc., 1983.

Stone, John Timothy. *Recruiting for Christ.* Westwood, N.J.: Revell, 1923.

Torrey, Ruben Archer. *How to Bring Men to Christ.* Minneapolis: Bethany House, 1977.

Trumbull, Charles G. *Taking Men Alive.* New York: Revell, 1938.

VanBaalen, J. K. *The Chaos of Cults.* Grand Rapids: Eerdmans Publishing Co., 1956.

INDEX